THINK ABOUT IT!

PHILOSOPHY

FOR KIDS

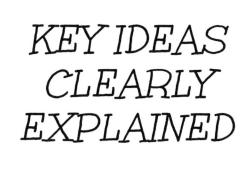

KEY IDEAS CLEARLY EXPLAINED

WRITTEN BY ALEX WOOLF

ARCTURUS

ARCTURUS

This edition published in 2021 by Arcturus Publishing Limited
26/27 Bickels Yard, 151–153 Bermondsey Street,
London SE1 3HA

Author: Alex Woolf
Illustrator: Jack Oliver Coles
Consultant: Dr. Daniel O'Brien
Designer: Stefan Holliland
Editors: Sebastian Rydberg and Laura Baker
Editorial Manager: Joe Harris
Design Manager: Jessica Holliland

ISBN: 978-1-83857-599-1
CH007401US
Supplier 42, Date 0121, Print run 9298

Printed in Singapore

CONTENTS

WHAT IS PHILOSOPHY?

Most of the time we go through our days not thinking very deeply about anything much. We might think things like, "Where is my next class?" or "I'm hungry," or, "This music sounds good!" We skim along the surface of life, experiencing its little pleasures and irritations, but we don't often question what life is actually all about.

Now and then, though, it's quite fun to take a step back from the daily hustle and bustle and look at things a bit more deeply. You may wonder, for example, why we are here. Or an even deeper question: Are we really here? If you ask yourself these sorts of questions, you're being a philosopher. And you're not alone. People have been asking themselves these kinds of questions for thousands of years.

What makes you "you"?

Philosophy was invented in ancient Greece. The word actually comes from two ancient Greek words: *philos*, meaning "love," and *sophos*, meaning "wisdom." So philosophy simply means "love of wisdom."

Philosophers seek answers to fundamental questions about themselves and the world they live in. That doesn't mean they ever find the truth. Philosophy is more like a never-ending conversation or debate that carries on through history. There may be no ultimate answers to the questions philosophers ask.

Does this tree exist only because Maria has thought of it? What happens when nobody is thinking of the tree?

How should we organize ourselves into "fair" societies? What is "fair"?

In this book, we look at some of the biggest questions philosophers have asked themselves, such as, "Is there such a thing as free will?" and, "Is your mind different from your body?" We'll also tackle some real puzzlers such as: "Can we be sure other people have minds?" Or, "Do numbers exist when no one's thinking about them?" If these questions leave you scratching your head, don't worry—some of the smartest people who've ever lived have also struggled with them!

WHAT IS KNOWLEDGE?

IN THE KNOW

The word "know" can mean many different things. Imagine a girl named Maria sitting in a classroom. Her friend Rahul is sitting next to her. She could say she *KNOWS* Rahul. That's one use of the word. Then Maria looks up and sees a photo of the city of Paris on the classroom wall. This reminds her that she *KNOWS* Paris because she took a trip there. That's another use of the word! And there are more ...

BUT DO YOU REALLY KNOW?

Suddenly, Harry, at the front of the class, puts up his hand. Maria just KNOWS Harry is about to ask a silly question—he's done it so many times in the past. But the teacher tells Harry to put his hand down for now, and he stays quiet. Maria was wrong. Sometimes we use the word "know" when we really mean "think," "believe," or "guess."

Next, the teacher tells everyone a fact. She says: "There are 206 bones in an adult human body." Now Maria KNOWS a fact about the human body.

KNOWING THAT

So that's four very different uses of the word "know"! Philosophers are most interested in knowing facts. They call this "declarative knowledge," or "knowledge-that." Here is an example: Maria is looking out of the window and KNOWS THAT it is snowing.

Declarative knowledge doesn't always have to use the phrase "KNOW THAT." It might have other wording, too. The most important thing is that what the person knows is a true fact. For example:

> Harry **knows how many** nuts there are in the bag.

> Jamila **knows where** her house is.

> Rahul **knows what** a chair is.

> Maria **knows when** the lesson is going to end.

HOW DO YOU KNOW?

Philosopher Bertrand Russell (1872–1970) talked about *knowledge by acquaintance* and *knowledge by description*. Knowledge by acquaintance is something you know from your direct experience: "I know that I have a headache."

Knowledge by description is knowledge you've learned indirectly from somewhere else: "I know that William Shakespeare wrote a play called *Romeo and Juliet*." You don't know this in the same way that you know you have a headache. An outside source, such as a teacher, told you about it.

KNOWING HOW

Another type of knowledge is "procedural knowledge," or "knowledge-how." Knowledge-that and knowledge-how are similar, but there are differences between the two, too. For example, someone might know all the facts about riding a bike. They might know that you must turn the pedals to go, and apply the brakes to stop, but that doesn't mean they KNOW HOW to ride a bike. That sort of knowledge doesn't come from facts, but from experience.

Anne knows HOW to ride a bike.

THE INGREDIENTS OF KNOWLEDGE

BELIEVE IT OR NOT

Saying "I *believe*" is not the same thing as saying "I *know*." Belief is something you think is true, but you can't prove it. It may be based on faith, or a hunch, or evidence from past experience. Rahul might believe there's a cat in the room, even though he hasn't seen it anywhere. He might remember, for example, that the cat is often in this room. It could be that this is the cat's feeding time. Rahul might have lots of reasons to believe the cat is in the room, but he can't say he *knows* it for a fact at the moment.

So, BELIEF is different from KNOWLEDGE. But, knowledge needs belief! To know something, you have to believe it. For example, you might have learned in class that an adult human has 206 bones, but if you don't believe it, then you can't say you know it.

TRUTH OF THE MATTER

On top of belief, the thing you know needs to be true. Say Jamila looks at her watch and sees it's 10:30. She checks with Harry to be sure. He checks his own watch and confirms that it is indeed 10:30. The evidence is clear. Their watches are in agreement. They BELIEVE it's 10:30. But what neither of them realize is that the clocks went back last night, and it's actually 9:30! Jamila and Harry might believe that it's 10:30, but they cannot say they know it because it isn't the true time. So, for something to be known, it must be both *believed* and *true.*

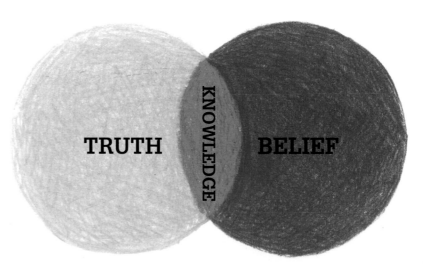

TRUTH   KNOWLEDGE   BELIEF

Truth and belief can exist separately, but knowledge needs both.

JUST GIVE ME A REASON

Is that it, then? Not quite! You might believe something, and it might also be true, but that doesn't necessarily make it knowledge. Rahul might believe there's a cat in the room, and this might be true. But that doesn't mean he KNOWS there is a cat in the room. For that, he needs one more thing: *justification*. In other words, he needs a good reason for holding this belief. If Rahul turns around and sees the cat, then he can say that he knows it for sure.

Of course it's possible that Rahul is still wrong. Maybe he just thinks he's seeing a cat, but it's something else, like a large hamster. Perhaps he's never seen a cat before and he just assumes that's what it is.

The stronger his justification for believing it's a cat, the more certain he can be in his knowledge.

THIS IS A CAT

So, now we have all the ingredients needed for knowledge—**belief**, **truth**, and **justification**. It was the ancient Greek philosopher **Plato** who first defined knowledge as justified true belief:

$$K = JTB.$$

This definition still holds up pretty well today.

WRESTLING WITH IDEAS: PLATO

Born to a wealthy family in Athens, in ancient Greece, Plato is one of most famous and influential philosophers of all time. You may even have heard his name before. But did you know that he was actually named Aristocles at birth? When he was young, his wrestling teacher gave him the nickname "Plato" (from *platos*, meaning "broad"), due to his big build. The name stuck!

FROM STUDENT TO TEACHER

As well as wrestling, Plato was fascinated by philosophy. He became a student of Socrates, the most celebrated philosopher of his day. Socrates never wrote anything down, so what we know of him comes from the writings of others—especially Plato. Socrates wandered around the city, challenging men to debate the meaning of things like courage, justice, and virtue. His skills were so great that the men he debated were often forced to change their opinions. Resentment against Socrates grew, and in 399 BCE he was tried and executed on a charge of "corrupting the youth."

Plato was deeply affected by Socrates' life and death and decided to devote his own life to philosophy. He wandered around Greece, Italy, and Egypt, picking up new ideas as he went. In the 380s BCE, he set up his Academy, a place of learning, much like a modern university. One of his students was Aristotle, the third of this great trio of classical Greek philosophers.

PUTTING PEN TO PAPER

Plato decided to write down what he'd learned from Socrates in the form of "dialogues." These were his own written versions of the debates that his master used to conduct in the streets and squares of Athens. Socrates was the main character in the dialogues, and in the early dialogues, the views and arguments that Plato's Socrates puts forward are very much based on the real Socrates. However, according to Aristotle, the "Socrates" of the later dialogues was actually Plato expressing his own ideas.

TRUE TO FORM

One of Plato's greatest contributions to philosophy was his idea of "forms." He believed that the world we live in—the "realm of the senses"—is an illusion. He described it as a mere image or copy of the real, unchanging world—the "realm of ideas," which we can access with our minds. So, for example, when we look at a dog, we are seeing an imperfect copy of the ideal form of a dog that we have in our minds. Dogs may take many different shapes and sizes here on Earth, but we recognize the essential doggy character they all share by comparing them to the ideal form.

Are these dogs just copies of an "ideal" dog?

Plato wrote about many other topics in philosophy, and his influence continues to this day. As British philosopher Alfred North Whitehead said, Western philosophy "consists of a series of footnotes to Plato." Plato's legacy lives on!

"If a man neglects education, he walks lame to the end of his life." — Plato

BEYOND BELIEF

WHEN IS A REASON JUSTIFICATION?

A person needs a reason to believe something. But is that enough? After all, there are good and bad reasons to believe things. It may be that some of the reasons we have for believing something just aren't good enough to be called justifications.

CHAIN REACTION

Philosophers are divided on this one. One group call themselves *foundationalists*. We'll take a closer look at them on pages 14–15. The other group are the *coherentists*. The coherentists say that a belief is justified if it agrees (or "coheres") with all the other beliefs a person holds. So, let's say that Maria believes that today is Tuesday. Her friend, Oliver, is a coherentist. Oliver would say that Maria's belief is justified on the basis of other beliefs that she holds, for example that yesterday was Monday and tomorrow is going to be Wednesday.

There is a problem with this though. Maria's belief may get its justification from other beliefs, but what are those beliefs based on? For example, Maria may believe that tomorrow is Wednesday based on the fact that Jamila told her so. But how can Maria justify her belief that Jamila didn't lie or

JUST A HUNCH

Harry might believe it's going to rain in ten minutes because he's seen a dark cloud in the sky. But Harry's no expert on the weather, so maybe that's not such a good justification on which to base his belief. And if the justification isn't any good, then you couldn't call Harry's belief knowledge—even if it does start raining in ten minutes! Feelings, hunches, and guesses cannot be justifications, however accurate they turn out to be. So what does count as a justification?

make a mistake? She will only be able to do so on the basis of yet more beliefs (about Jamila's character, for example), and these, in turn, will also need justifying.

This is the argument against coherentism—it relies on the support of a long chain of other beliefs to make it work. This chain may be endless or it may even circle back on itself. But a coherentist like Oliver would argue that this isn't a problem. He would say it isn't an endless chain or circle at all, but a web with lots of interconnecting strands. Each belief supports the other beliefs in the web, all helping to strengthen the justification of Maria's central belief that today is Tuesday.

EVIDENCE OF THE SENSES

Another argument against coherentism is that not all our beliefs are based on a web of other beliefs. A lot of them are based on simply SENSING things. For example, if Rahul touches a hot plate, his belief that the plate is hot isn't based on lots of other beliefs about plates or hotness. He believes the plate is hot because he can feel it. Coherentism seems to ignore the fact that many of our beliefs are based on just one justification—the evidence of our senses.

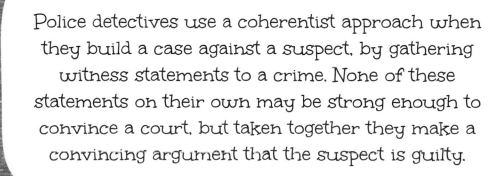

Police detectives use a coherentist approach when they build a case against a suspect, by gathering witness statements to a crime. None of these statements on their own may be strong enough to convince a court, but taken together they make a convincing argument that the suspect is guilty.

BACK TO BASICS

CAN KNOWLEDGE HAVE FIRM FOUNDATIONS?

Is it possible to have a belief that isn't based on any other belief—a belief so basic that no one can say it isn't true? *Foundationalists* think so. What's more, they think that these *BASIC BELIEFS* should form the foundation and justification of all other beliefs. That, they say, is the only way to build a firm foundation for knowledge.

CRASHING DOWN

Foundationalists don't agree that a web of beliefs leads to justification. They suggest that if all these beliefs rely on each other for justification, it's like building a house without a foundation. The whole structure could collapse!

BASIC BELIEF TYPES

Foundationalists divide basic beliefs into three main types:

1. Beliefs founded on reason or logic, such as, "Oliver believes that two plus three equals five."

2. Beliefs about experiences of the mind, such as, "Maria believes she is in pain." Even though it could be possible that Maria might be wrong about where she feels the pain, or what's causing it (non-basic beliefs), most foundationalists would consider her belief that she is in pain to be a basic belief.

3. Beliefs about experiences of the senses, such as, "Maria believes she hears sounds," or, "Jamila believes she sees something red." You might notice that these are quite general and vague. In contrast, if you said, "Maria believes she hears a Mozart symphony," or "Jamila believes she sees a rose," these would be non-basic beliefs, because Maria and Jamila could be making a mistake.

THE PROBLEM IS …

Foundationalists often disagree about what a basic belief is. Oliver says a basic belief can be based only on reason or logic (e.g. two plus three equals five). This makes Oliver a *rationalist*. Maria, on the other hand, says a basic belief can be founded only on the experiences of the mind and the senses. This makes Maria an *empiricist*.

Another even more serious problem with foundationalism is that it's not always clear how we should use basic beliefs to justify the trickier non-basic beliefs. For example, how do we go from "Jamila believes she sees something red," to, "Jamila believes she sees a rose"? There are not very many basic beliefs to build on, so we are left with quite a limited number of things we can call justifiable beliefs.

For these reasons, many foundationalists today are less strict than traditional (classical) foundationalists. Today's "modest foundationalists" might, for example, include a recent memory as a basic belief, such as, "Rahul believes he ate cereal for breakfast this morning." This is something classical foundationalists would reject, because memories are not always accurate.

Test your own beliefs! Think of things you believe to be true. Do you believe that eggs break when you drop them? That there is milk in your fridge? That bees die after they sting you? That stealing is wrong? Something else? **What are these beliefs based on? Reason? Experience? Other beliefs?**

You might learn about yourself and what kind of philosopher you are when you examine your justifications.

THE GETTIER PROBLEM

DOES JUSTIFIED TRUE BELIEF ALWAYS EQUAL KNOWLEDGE?

K = JTB *seems* to be true in almost all cases—but there is one exception. In 1963, an American philosopher named Edmund Gettier pointed out that in some situations you can have a justified true belief in something, but you still can't call it knowledge. There might be something else involved ...

JUST MY LUCK

Gettier gave the example of two people, Smith and Jones, who apply for the same job. As they are waiting to be interviewed, Smith recognizes Jones. He saw him at another interview earlier that week. He remembers that Jones lent him two coins to buy a coffee. Smith takes this opportunity to repay Jones the two coins he owes him.

Later, during Smith's interview, the president of the company tells him that he is going to offer the job to Jones. Hearing this, Smith concludes that the man who will get the job has two coins in his pocket. He is justified in this belief because he saw Jones put the coins in his pocket just ten minutes ago.

Suddenly, the president changes his mind and offers the job to Smith. Then Smith discovers that, by coincidence, he also has two coins in his pocket. So Smith had been right that the man who got the job had two coins in his pocket. Through sheer luck, his justified belief turned out to be true—but you couldn't call it knowledge.

This is known as the Gettier Problem. How can *K = JTB* if it turns out to be true through luck and coincidence?

FEELING SHEEPISH

Take another example. Jamila is walking through the countryside when she sees a sheep in a field. Jamila has a justified belief (based on the evidence of her eyesight) that there is a sheep in the field. She decides to walk over to the sheep. As she gets closer, she discovers that it isn't a sheep at all. It's a white rock shaped like a sheep. Her eyes were playing tricks on her!

As she's getting over her surprise, a real sheep suddenly steps out from behind the rock. So there is a sheep in the field after all! Her justified belief was true. Yet when she first formed that belief, she couldn't say she KNEW there was a sheep in the field.

The Gettier Problem has forced philosophers to look again at *K = JTB*. Some say Gettier hasn't proved it's wrong because the beliefs in his cases aren't fully justified. Smith, for example, should have known the company's president might change his mind. Others accept the problem and say the formula needs to be revised. They suggest there should be a fourth condition for something to count as knowledge. In other words, *K = JTB + ?* Philosophers have yet to agree on what that fourth condition should be.

Do you think **K = JTB** should be revised because of the Gettier Problem? Would you add a fourth condition? If so, what should that condition be?

DIVIDING OPINION: DAVID HUME

David Hume grew up in Ninewells, Scotland, in a family with noble ancestry but little money. His father died when he was two, and Hume and his brother and sister were brought up and educated by their mother. Hume was extremely bright and went to Edinburgh University when he was just twelve. He thought about a career in law, but when he was eighteen he discovered the joy of philosophy.

AUTHOR ON THE MOVE

In 1739, at the age of twenty-three, Hume wrote his first book of philosophy, *A Treatise of Human Nature*. The book received very poor reviews at the time, but is now considered one of the most important works in the history of Western philosophy.

Hume lived in many European cities and did various jobs during his life, including tutor, secretary, diplomat, and librarian. He applied to become a professor of philosophy at Edinburgh University but was rejected because people thought he didn't believe in God. During his life, he wrote many books, including further works of philosophy and a best-selling, six-volume *History of England*.

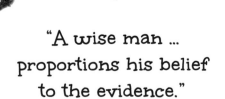

"A wise man ... proportions his belief to the evidence."
– David Hume

FORK IN THE ROAD

In his *Treatise of Human Nature*, Hume divided knowledge into two categories, which he called *demonstrative statements* and *probable statements*. A demonstrative statement is one that is obviously true or false, such as, "Two plus three equals five," (true) or, "One plus four equals seven," (false). Probable statements are not obviously true or false. They need the evidence of our senses to say whether they're true or not. A probable statement might be, "Harry is in the kitchen." You'd need to go into the kitchen to see if it was correct. Dividing statements into these two categories is often called *Hume's fork*.

Hume had a concern about probable statements though. For example, take the probable statement, "The sun will rise tomorrow." We are assuming an event will happen based on evidence of our senses of past events. But how can we be sure the future will be the same as the past? It's impossible for us to experience a future event with our senses.

CAUSE AND EFFECT

Hume makes a similar claim for cause-and-effect situations. For example, if Anne lets go of a plate, then the plate will fall to the ground. Hume claims this is neither demonstrative nor probable. Just because in the past plates have always fallen to the ground when we let go of them doesn't mean they always will, or that the letting go is what causes the falling to the ground. He gives the example of two clocks set a few seconds apart. One always chimes a few seconds after the other. Just because these events always follow each other doesn't mean the one causes the other.

Hume's conclusion is that we can't use reason as a basis for knowledge—we can only use belief and custom. In other words, we can only say it is *probable* that the sun will rise tomorrow and that a plate will fall when you drop it, because this is what has happened in the past.

IS IT ALL AN ILLUSION?

DO WE REALLY KNOW ANYTHING?

We've talked about what knowledge is and what it isn't. But all along we've assumed that knowledge actually exists—that it's possible to know things. Some philosophers have questioned even that assumption. They are known as *skeptics*. One of the first skeptics was Socrates, who said that the only thing he knew for sure was that he knew nothing. René Descartes (see pages 22–23) also used skeptical theories in his arguments.

JUST A DREAM

How do the skeptics justify this idea that you can't know anything for certain? Surely we can gain knowledge through our senses, for example? We can pick up an apple, bite into it, and gather information about it through touch, taste, and smell. But skeptics say: "How do you know you're not dreaming about the apple?" They remind us that while we dream, we don't actually know we're dreaming. It's only after we wake up that we realize it. So how do we know we won't one day wake up from what we think of as real life and discover that's all been a dream, too?

This is a difficult argument to disprove, but many philosophers have tried, mainly by pointing out that the experience of dreams is very different to that of waking life. John Locke said you can't experience pain in dreams. However, modern scientific studies have shown that pain *is* actually possible in dreams, though it's not as severe as in real life.

In 1959, the American philosopher Norman Malcolm claimed that it makes no sense to say that we could be thinking in a dream. If we're thinking, we must be awake.

BRAIN GAMES

Skeptics also use the *brain-in-a-vat* argument. Imagine an evil scientist has removed Rahul's brain from his body and placed it in a vat of life-sustaining fluid. The scientist has connected his brain by wires to a computer. The computer sends electrical impulses into Rahul's brain so that it can see, hear, smell, taste, and touch, just as in real life. The brain has perfectly normal, conscious experiences just like Rahul would have in his body, and it isn't able to tell it's actually in a vat.

Skeptics say that even though the brain-in-a-vat idea is extremely unlikely, we can't completely rule it out. Therefore, logically, we can't say for certain that we know anything. It could all be simulated like this.

Philosophers have struggled to disprove this argument. They've pointed out that a

brain in a vat experiences the world fundamentally differently than a brain in a body, which senses things with all parts of its external body. But skeptics answer that the scientist could adapt the machine to allow for that difference—maybe it could be a body in a vat, for example? The debate continues!

The imaginary brain in a vat receives experiences from a computer.

How would you feel if you learned that the external world is just a simulation and you are, in fact, a brain in a vat? Would it make any difference? Would it change the way you behaved? Perhaps all that matters to you is that the world feels real. Or perhaps the reality of life gives meaning to you, and if you found out it was all fake, you couldn't enjoy it any more.

In that case, would you rather be told you were a brain in a vat, or never know the truth?

PLANTING DOUBT: RENÉ DESCARTES

René Descartes was born near Tours, France. In 1619, while serving as a soldier, he had a series of dreams or visions. He claimed these revealed to him a new kind of philosophy based on mathematics, and he became determined to pursue this. He studied philosophy, mathematics, and science, and came up with a new way of doing philosophy based on deductive reasoning (using logic to reach a conclusion). Ever since, he's been called *the father of modern philosophy*.

STRIP IT BACK

In one of his most famous works, *Meditations on First Philosophy* (1641), Descartes aimed to show that even if we start from an extremely skeptical point of view, doubting everything, we can still prove that knowledge exists. To do this, Descartes developed a system called the *method of doubt*. He used this method to strip away, layer by layer, all his certainties about the world. First, he rejected knowledge learned from books and teachings. Then he cast aside the evidence of his senses because these senses often tricked him. For example, if he placed a stick in water, it would look bent, even though it was straight.

Next, Descartes wondered if he could even be sure that he was sitting in his study. He decided he must doubt this, too, as he might be dreaming. Then he said, "Okay, maybe I'm dreaming, but mathematics has got to be real, right? Two plus three equals five, even in a dream!"

But Descartes decided that even this was open to doubt. Perhaps God had created people in a way that caused us to make errors in our reasoning—so we cannot rely on mathematics. And speaking of God, could Descartes even be sure that he existed, or the world he supposedly created? Perhaps Descartes was under the control of an evil demon that had made him think there was an external world, when in fact it was all an illusion.

Is it all an illusion?

ALL ABOUT ME!

Descartes' method seemed to take him to an impossible position where he was forced to doubt everything. And that's when it hit him—who was doing the doubting? The one thing he could never doubt was his own existence. It even passed the evil demon test—the demon could only make him believe he existed if he did, in fact, exist. Descartes called this his *First Certainty*, and he expressed it in one of philosophy's most famous phrases: "I think, therefore I am."

The First Certainty saved Descartes from getting sucked into a spiral of never-ending doubt. It allowed him to start his journey from skepticism back to knowledge.

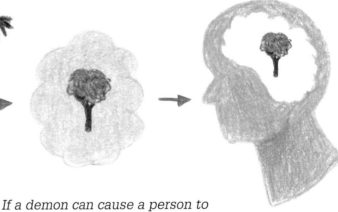

If a demon can cause a person to doubt, that person must exist to do the doubting!

"Some evil demon of utmost power and cunning has employed all his energies to deceive me ... I shall consider myself as not having hands or eyes, or flesh, or blood, or senses, but as falsely believing that I have all these things." — René Descartes

WHATEVER WORKS

DOES IT MATTER IF WE DON'T KNOW ANYTHING?

Philosophers have been asking questions about knowledge since ancient times. But in the end, why do any of these things matter? Surely all we should care about is that this stuff that's in our heads, which we call knowledge, helps us get through our lives. We turn a handle, it opens a door. We flick a switch, a light comes on. Call it knowledge, call it whatever you like, the important thing is that it works!

TOOL OF THE TRADE

This is the attitude of a group of philosophers called *pragmatists*. As far as they're concerned, knowledge is nothing more than a practical tool to help us overcome the problems of life. They don't see knowledge as universal and unchanging. For each person it can be different, depending on their situation. For example, a tourist's knowledge of Paris would be different from that of someone who lives and works there.

IT GOES BOTH WAYS

Pragmatists don't see knowledge as something separate from ourselves that existed before we knew it. For them, gaining knowledge is not like pouring water into a glass. They see it more as a two-way process between the knowledge and the person receiving it. When you learn tennis, for example, your body isn't just passively receiving a skill—the knowledge you acquire is affected by your particular body and mind. Anne and Harry might both know how to play tennis, but that doesn't mean their knowledge of tennis is identical. Both know and play it in slightly different ways.

Think about how scientists discover new things about the world. They don't read it from a great book of knowledge. They don't download it from a computer. They do it by experimenting in laboratories, or by looking through telescopes at the stars, or by digging for fossils. Gaining knowledge is an active process, and by deciding what experiments to do, or choosing what part of the sky to look at, the knowledge-seekers affect the knowledge they gain.

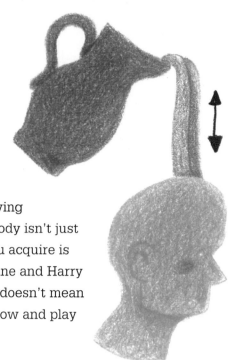

Learning is not like pouring water into an empty vessel—because your mind is anything but empty. The knowledge-seeker affects the knowledge, just as the knowledge affects the knowledge-seeker.

HOPE AND EXPECTATION

In our daily lives, we're often actively seeking knowledge. Jamila wants to know where Rahul is. She thinks he's in the clothes store, so she goes in and, sure enough, there he is. Now she knows where Rahul is. In gaining this knowledge, she was guided by her hope (finding Rahul) and her expectation (she knew he liked this store).

For pragmatists, knowledge isn't some abstract thing. It's practical and adaptable. It comes from solving problems in order to achieve our hopes and ambitions.

According to pragmatist philosopher William James (1842–1910), the essence of pragmatism is "**what works best in a particular situation.**"

IS THERE A "ME"?

HOW CAN WE BE SURE WE EXIST?

Every day I get up, eat, go out, work, have fun, sleep. When I look in the mirror, I see a person looking back who is, apparently, me. But how can I be sure I really exist? David Hume suggested that we never actually experience our own self, just a continuous chain of experiences. On a walk, we might feel the breeze on our face, smell the scent of wild flowers, and hear the sound of birdsong, and we may think, "That's me experiencing all that." But how can we be certain?

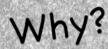 Why?

 ???

 How?

THINKERS AND THOUGHTS

What about René Descartes' First Certainty: I think, therefore I am? Is even that enough to prove our existence beyond doubt? After all, what or who is this *"I"* he talks about? How does he know there's a thinker at all? Maybe thoughts just exist on their own without any need for a thinker. It's a very strange idea, but a skeptic would say it's possible.

IT STANDS TO REASON …

The problem with the theory that thoughts could exist without thinkers is that it doesn't allow for the existence of reasoning. For reasoning to happen, someone or something needs to take these thoughts and put them together. For example, here are two thoughts:

1. All tennis players use rackets.
2. Anne is a tennis player.

Putting these two thoughts together, we can use reason to work out a third thought:

3. Anne uses a racket.

If the two thoughts existed independently, there couldn't be any connection between them. It takes a thinker to put them together and use reason to produce the third thought. Therefore, thinkers must exist.

Descartes himself used a similar form of reasoning to reach his First Certainty. It went like this:

1. I think.
2. Anything that thinks must exist.
3. Therefore I exist.

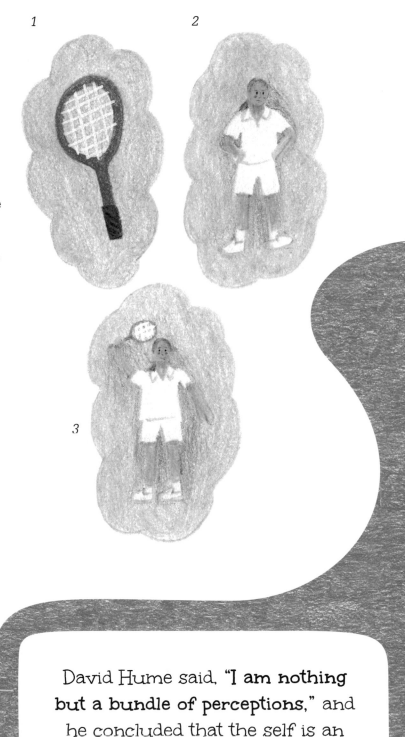

FACT OR FICTION?

Some critics have found a flaw in this reasoning. The second statement says: *"Anything that thinks must exist."* J.K. Rowling describes Harry Potter as thinking, so does that mean Harry Potter exists? Of course not! Harry Potter is a fictional character who doesn't exist in the real world. But then who's to say we're not all fictional characters in a world created by an unknown author? In the "real world" of that author, we wouldn't exist either. Descartes has an answer to this criticism, and it lies in his use of the first person, "I." When he said, "I think, therefore I am," he was only talking about himself. He was saying that he exists to himself, in his own universe, just as Harry Potter would exist to himself in the world of Hogwarts.

David Hume said, **"I am nothing but a bundle of perceptions,"** and he concluded that the self is an illusion. **What do you think?**

MIND OVER MATTER: GEORGE BERKELEY

Have you ever wondered whether the world exists when you're not looking at it? This was the question pondered by Irish philosopher George Berkeley. In fact, he went so far as to say that nothing exists, except in the minds of its perceivers. Berkeley was an *empiricist*, meaning that he saw experience as the main source of knowledge. His form of empiricism was very extreme—he believed that there's only one substance in the universe, and that substance is mind. Matter doesn't exist except as an idea in the minds of those who perceive it.

LIFE STORY

Berkeley was born and raised at Dysart Castle near Kilkenny in Ireland. He went to school at Kilkenny College before entering Trinity College, Dublin, at the age of fifteen. In 1710, he was ordained as a priest, and by 1714, aged 29, he'd written his most famous philosophical works. After that, he journeyed around Europe, returning to Ireland in 1724 where he became Dean of Derry. Berkeley tried to found a seminary (a school for priests) in Bermuda, but couldn't raise enough funds. In 1734, he became Bishop of Cloyne, Dublin, where he remained for the rest of his life.

Is this a vase or just an image of a vase in Oliver's mind?

PERCEPTION AND REALITY

To understand how Berkeley reached his conclusion that nothing exists except the mind, let's use an example. When Oliver looks at a vase, it starts a chain of events in his body. First, an image of the vase appears in the retinas of his eyes. Then, this image is transmitted in the form of electrical signals, via his optic nerve, to his brain. Finally, the brain puts the image back together from these electrical signals. What Oliver sees, therefore, is not the actual vase, but a reconstruction of it in his mind. The image of the vase is, in this sense, no different from an image in his mind formed during a dream, and it might be just as removed from reality. Oliver has no way of knowing if the actual vase is anything like the image in his mind.

According to Berkeley, all our perceptions of the world—whether they are sights, sounds, smells, tastes, or textures — are formed in our minds, and we can never know if they resemble reality at all. So if we never perceive the material world directly, but only as ideas in our mind, we can't assume that it exists, as it is never actually being perceived.

A MATTER OF PERCEPTION

Critics found Berkeley's ideas absurd. They said, if there's no material world outside of our ideas, then how do things continue to exist when no one's around to perceive them? Would that mean that when someone closes their bedroom door, their bedroom ceases to exist? Surely not! Bishop Berkeley had an answer to this: God perceives things at all times, he said, so the empty bedroom continues to be perceived in the mind of God.

Do I exist?

Yes!

For Berkeley, things can continue to exist when no one sees them, because God perceives them.

"To be is to be perceived."
– George Berkeley

SOMETHING OR NOTHING?

DOES "NOTHING" EXIST?

Try closing your eyes and thinking of nothing. It's hard, isn't it? When we're awake, we're always thinking of something, even if what we're thinking about is the idea of nothing! So does nothing exist? If it does, it belongs to the world of *concepts*: things you can't see or touch, but that exist as a concept, like Friday, or fairies, or philosophy. We often think of nothing as the absence of something, or a space where there could be something. For example, there's nothing in my cup, but there might be juice in there later.

WHY BOTHER?

Many philosophers have pondered the concept of nothingness—what it is and whether it exists. One of the earliest to do so was Parmenides, a Greek philosopher of the fifth century BCE (see pages 34–35). He argued that if you think or talk about something, it has to be something that exists. Even if the thing you're talking or thinking about is in the past, it must still exist in some sense now. So if everything we can speak of exists, there can't be such a thing as non-existence, or nothing.

Another ancient Greek philosopher, Democritus (*c.* 460–371 BCE), disagreed with Parmenides. Democritus was an *atomist*. He believed that all matter was composed of tiny particles called atoms. In Democritus' view, nature was made up entirely of either atoms or void (the space through which the atoms moved). To him, the void was entirely empty. It was "nothing."

Aristotle saw it slightly differently again—space, he said, was a container for matter. In other words, it was SOMETHING rather than nothing. As for the void, he dismissed it as not even worthy of discussion. If it doesn't exist, he argued, why bother with it?

THE "HOLE" PICTURE

An interesting example of the problem of nothingness is the idea of a hole. What exactly is a hole? Is it something, or is it nothing? The hole in a bagel is made of nothing. Yet without it, the bagel would look quite different. There would be more bagel for a start! A hole in the bottom of a bucket is also made of nothing, yet by being there it makes the bucket completely useless for carrying water.

Some philosophers say that holes don't exist—you can only speak of *holed objects*. So you can say, "This is a holed bucket," but not, "This bucket has a hole in it." If this were true, it might cause problems with language—for example, how could you compare two different-sized holes in a carpet if you're not allowed to refer to holes as things?

Another theory is that what we're talking about when we say "hole" isn't the space part, but the surrounding part—the interior of the bagel ring, for example. But does this really capture what a hole is? If you take a coin and place it inside the circle of a bagel, you could say that the coin is inside the hole of the bagel and people will understand you. But if the hole is just the surrounding surface, that statement makes no sense.

So it turns out holes are not as simple as they might first appear. The same goes for the whole subject of nothingness.

It's fine! Holes don't exist!

The concept of zero came surprisingly late to mathematics. To write the number 204, the ancient Sumerians would leave an empty space instead of a zero. Zero was also never used alone. If you asked an ancient mathematician what three minus three was, they wouldn't have been able to answer!

Zero was finally invented in India around the fifth century.

CONSTANT CHANGE

DO WE LIVE IN A WORLD OF CHANGE?

When we look at the world, it seems like a place that's always changing. The sun rises and sets, the moon waxes and wanes, the tides come in and out, spring changes to summer, and fall to winter. Hot things grow cool, wet things become dry, living things are born, and they grow old and die. Everything is changing, and nothing is ever fixed. Or is it?

FINDING BALANCE

Change was key to the beliefs of the ancient Greek philosopher Heraclitus (c.535–475 BCE). The only permanent thing in the universe, according to Heraclitus, was change. He viewed the universe as a constant battle for dominance between competing elements. The elements, he said, were fire, water, and earth. Fire came first and gave rise to the other two, which are its opposites. Everything, claimed Heraclitus, was made from a mixture of these three elements.

He saw a tension between fire and its opposites. Sometimes one dominated, and sometimes the others. This, he said, was what caused the changes around us, such as day changing to night and winter to summer. A balance of strength between these competing elements ensures that one never dominates for long.

Take a look at a bow (from a bow and arrow), said Heraclitus. The tension of the string keeps the curved shape of the bow in place. This is the perfect example of tension leading to harmony.

THE SAME BUT DIFFERENT

Heraclitus famously said, "You can never step in the same river twice." In other words, each time you step into a river, you are washed by different waters, yet the river itself is always described as one unchanging thing.

In another example, he said, "The road up and the road down are one and the same." Even though the road itself is the same, it can be very different, depending on which direction you travel. At its core, Heraclitus' message is that when we think about the universe, we shouldn't think of it as a single substance, but as a process.

Heraclitus saw this never-ending process of change taking place in human beings, too. He believed the soul was a mixture of fire and water. Fire was the noble part that could be weakened by "watery" elements such as laziness, stupidity, and wickedness. Worldly pleasures, according to Heraclitus, made the soul moist and ought to be resisted.

Heraclitus' views echo the yin and yang of ancient Chinese philosophy. Chinese philosophers believed that all of nature could be divided into two fundamental forces—yin and yang.

They saw all aspects of nature occurring from this duality, including light and dark, fire and water, winter and summer, and male and female.

Yin and yang

RESISTING CHANGE: PARMENIDES

In contrast to Heraclitus, the ancient Greek philosopher Parmenides of Elea declared that there is no such thing as change or non-existence at all. He believed that everything that exists has always existed and will always exist. To reach this conclusion, he used the new technique of *deductive reasoning*.

NON-EXISTING NON-EXISTENCE

Parmenides argued that if we can think of a unicorn, a unicorn must therefore exist, even if only in our minds. So if anything we can think of exists, it can't also NOT exist. Therefore, non-existence is impossible (see pages 30–31).

Reality, then, is not how it appears to be. Unicorns, Harry Potter, and Martians all exist! In fact, for Parmenides, EVERYTHING exists and is all part of a single unified substance. This position is called *monism*.

IMPOSSIBLE CHANGE

By this same logic, Parmenides also declared that change is impossible. If you can think of something that existed in the past, then it still exists in your mind now. Maria can call to mind her pet hamster, even though it died months ago, and so the hamster in some sense still exists. Similarly, if Jamila decides to compose a song, that song exists as an idea in her mind before it is created. In other words, everything exists, whether in the past, present, or future. Nothing can come into existence or pass out of existence. Change, therefore, is an illusion.

There is a problem, though, with Parmenides' reasoning. It lies with the meaning of the word "exist." He is saying that existing in the world is the same sort of thing as existing in the mind. Many philosophers question this assumption.

Even so, Parmenides was highly influential and did get everyone thinking about the complicated nature of existence, and the differences between thoughts, words, and objects.

UNMOVING MOTION

One of Parmenides' main followers was Zeno of Elea. Zeno said that if change was impossible, so was motion, and he tried to show this with a thought experiment. He said, "Imagine an arrow being fired." Then, he pointed out that the time it takes for the arrow to reach its target can be broken down into a series of instants. At each of these instants, the arrow is motionless. If the arrow is motionless at each instant, and time is made up of instants, then motion is impossible. Do you agree?

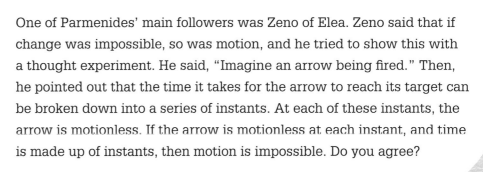

"We can speak and think only of what exists.
And what exists is uncreated and imperishable
for it is whole and unchanging and complete."
— Parmenides of Elea

THE SHIP OF THESEUS

HOW MUCH CAN SOMETHING CHANGE AND STILL BE THE SAME THING?

In ancient Greece, the legendary king Theseus won many battles for the city of Athens. When he died, the citizens decided to keep his ship in the port to remember their great ruler. As time went by, the planks of the Ship of Theseus started to rot and had to be replaced. The craftspeople were careful to replace the parts with the same kind of timber, and to use the same shipbuilding techniques as the original ship. Gradually, more and more of the ship was replaced until, after several centuries, no part of the original ship remained.

BOATLOAD OF QUESTIONS

The question for philosophers is this: Is the repaired ship still the "Ship of Theseus," or is it now a different ship? If you think it's a different ship, when did it stop being the Ship of Theseus? After the first plank was replaced? After more than half of the ship was replaced? After the final part was replaced?

If you think it's the same ship, would it have made a difference if all the parts were replaced at once instead of over hundreds of years? If you think the change has to be gradual, how gradual should it be? Is ten years all right? Ten months? Ten weeks?

These questions have been debated for centuries, ever since the Ship of Theseus problem was first put forward by philosophers such as Heraclitus and Plato.

IDENTIFYING IDENTITY

It all comes down to a question of identity. What exactly is a physical object, and how much can it change before it becomes something different? Heraclitus believed that the ship was both the same and different. Aristotle believed that it was the same ship because the purpose and design didn't change.

There are plenty more questions we can ask to further challenge our idea of what an object is. What would happen if you replaced the old wooden planks with planks of plastic or metal, gradually changing the ship into a different material? What if the craftspeople made mistakes and put the new parts in wrongly? What if the ship could no longer float or sail because of these changes?

WHICH SHIP IS WHICH?

The philosopher Thomas Hobbes asked a different question. Imagine that each time a part of the ship was replaced, the original part was stored in a warehouse. Over time, all the original parts were restored to good condition and assembled into a ship that looked exactly like the original ship. Now, which of the two ships should be called the Ship of Theseus— the one with the replaced parts, or the one rebuilt from the old parts?

People go both ways on the question of which ship is which. Some modern philosophers say the ships are separate concepts in the human mind and cannot be the same at all.

What do you think?

INFLUENCING THOUGHT: IMMANUEL KANT

Immanuel Kant was born in the city of Königsberg, Prussia. He studied philosophy, physics, and mathematics at the city's university and went on to teach there. In his fifties and sixties he published a series of philosophical works that made him famous around the world, including *A Critique of Pure Reason* (1781) and *A Critique of Practical Reason* (1788). Kant has probably had more influence on philosophy than anyone since Aristotle.

TIME TO EXIST

In *A Critique of Pure Reason*, Kant said that for something to exist, it must be located in time. In other words, we must be able to say WHEN it exists and for HOW LONG. The trouble is, our consciousness is hard to locate in time because we experience it as just a series of "nows." We can only measure time by comparing these internal "nows" to external things that move or change.

Kant gave the example of a clock. Looking at the hands alone tells you nothing. You need to see them moving past the numbers on the clock face to tell the time. Similarly, when we watch a sunrise, we can measure our internal, changing "now" against something in the world. For Kant, this was a way of demonstrating both his own existence, and that of the external world.

INTUITIONS AND UNDERSTANDING

Kant also looked at the question of how we experience the world. He decided there were two elements to it. The first he called "intuitions." This is our direct experience of individual things in time and space. For example, Maria looks at an old oak tree.

Kant called the second element "understanding." This is our ability to experience concepts such as "tree." If Maria didn't have a concept of "tree," she wouldn't know her intuition was of an old oak tree. And without such intuitions, she wouldn't know there were such things as trees at all. So intuitions give us experience of particular things, while understanding gives us experience of general concepts.

Maria has an intuition and an understanding of the concept of an oak tree.

ROSE-TINTED GLASSES

We know that when a tree's leaves change from green to brown, the tree is still the same tree.

Some of what Kant calls "understanding" comes from previous experiences, and some of it comes from *a priori* knowledge: Things we know without having to experience them. Kant believed that our understanding of things like space, time, and substance all come from a priori knowledge. If we didn't have this knowledge, he said, we would think that when a tree's leaves changed from green to brown, it had become a different tree.

Imagine you are wearing pink sunglasses. Everything appears pink. So you will know a priori that everything you look at will appear pink. For Kant, it's as though our minds have similar filters that make it so we always see the world in terms of space and time relations and things causing other things to happen. We can't help but see the world this way, so this knowledge is a priori. That's because of how our minds work. How the world is IN ITSELF is something we can't know about. He called his philosophy *transcendental idealism*.

"All our knowledge begins with the senses, proceeds then to the understanding, and ends with reason. There is nothing higher than reason."
— Immanuel Kant

JUGGLING NUMBERS

DO NUMBERS EXIST?

Think of a number. Add three. Double that. Subtract four. Divide that by two. Subtract your original number. The answer should be one! You did all that in your head, right? You played around with numbers in your head just like a circus performer juggling bowling pins. But what exactly were you juggling? Numbers aren't like bowling pins. You can't actually pick them up to juggle them, yet they seem real. If they weren't, you couldn't have done the above exercise. They seem to exist in a world between the real and the unreal.

NEED FOR NUMBERS

Numbers fall into a category that philosophers call *abstract objects*. These are things that appear to exist, but can't be found in space and time. Other examples of abstract objects are lines, triangles, the direction north, and Alice in Wonderland. Here we're not talking about a particular copy of *Alice in Wonderland*—that would be a physical object. We're talking about the concept or idea of that book. If you destroyed every existing copy of *Alice in Wonderland,* the idea of it would still exist in our minds.

But numbers aren't really like novels. Novels are written by humans, whereas numbers have always been there. Numbers had to be discovered by humans, probably because they needed them. Early farmers, for example, needed to know how many cattle or goats they had, so they developed a system of counting.

MORE THAN COUNTING

In this sense, numbers began not as abstract objects but as "properties." A property is a characteristic of something. For example, redness might be a property of an apple. In the same way, four might be a property of a group of apples. Properties aren't physical. You can touch a red apple, but you can't touch the redness on its own. You can touch the group of apples, but you can't touch the "fourness" on its own. Numbers as properties don't always have to apply to physical objects. You can make five trips to a museum or be granted three wishes by a genie.

Numbers may have begun as simple tools for counting, but they soon became much more than that. Humans figured out that they could add or subtract one set of numbers to or from another. Later still, they worked out multiplication, division, geometry, trigonometry, algebra, calculus, and many other techniques of mathematics. All these methods of manipulating numbers were discovered by different people at different times, so you can't say they were created like a novel. They, like numbers, must have existed in an abstract sense before humans discovered them.

Like unicorns, numbers can be thought about, but they have no physical existence. Of course, you could write a number down, but that's like drawing a unicorn—it's just a representation of something, and not the real thing.

CAUSE AND EFFECT

DOES EVERYTHING HAVE A CAUSE?

Harry kicks the ball high into the air. It hits the kitchen window, smashing it. The ball caused the window to break, right? Common sense would say yes. Harry's dad comes outside. He's angry. It looks like Harry might be in trouble. But wait … here comes a philosopher! She witnessed the incident, and she might be able to stick up for Harry.

Is Harry's dad right to be angry that Harry caused the window to break?

JUST COMMON SENSE

The philosopher says: "I saw Harry kick the ball, the ball strike the window, and the window break. What I didn't see was the ball CAUSING the window to break. Nor did I see the window breaking as an EFFECT of the ball striking it. Causes and effects aren't objects any of us can see, so it's very hard to prove they're real."

"But it's common sense," fumes Harry's dad, "that the ball caused the window to break."

"For centuries," says the philosopher, "it seemed like common sense that the Sun revolved around the Earth, but it didn't. I'm not saying you're wrong. It seems very likely that the window didn't just break spontaneously. I just need something more than common sense to prove to me the ball was the cause."

CLAIMING CORRELATION

So Harry's dad says: "If my son kicked a thousand balls at a thousand windows and broke all of them, would that be enough to convince you that the ball caused the window to break?"

The philosopher shakes her head. "That would certainly be a strong correlation," she says. Seeing Harry's puzzled face, she explains: "A *correlation* is when two kinds of things occur together. But correlation is not the same as *causality*, which says that the cause directly created the effect."

WHAT'S THE VERDICT?

"So where exactly does that leave me?" asks Harry. "Am I guilty or innocent?"

The philosopher replies: "I tend to agree with David Hume and Immanuel Kant on this one. Both accepted that causality couldn't be proved in the world in itself, BUT they also saw it as essential to the way human beings make sense of the world. So, the connection between the ball hitting the window and the window breaking lies in the way the mind interprets these two events, not in the events themselves. We as humans have no way of interpreting the world except with our minds. And that means, I'm afraid, that you're going to have to take responsibility for the broken window after all!"

Why isn't **correlation** the same as **causality**? Let's look at an example. In a coastal town, the number of surfing accidents is **correlated** with ice cream sales—whenever surfing accidents go up, so do ice cream sales. Does this mean that injured surfers comfort themselves with frozen treats? Not necessarily. It's more likely that both numbers go up during the summer months. This is correlation, not cause.

THE MEANING OF LIFE

DOES LIFE HAVE A MEANING?

Have you ever wondered why you're here? What purpose or meaning your life has, other than to simply survive? If so, you aren't alone. A group of philosophers called *existentialists* have pondered these questions. Many of them conclude that the universe IS meaningless, but that we should not despair—we should embrace our existence and try to find the meaning we want in life.

Heidegger said that without knowing about death, our lives would have no meaning.

WORLD DOMINATION

German philosopher Friedrich Nietzsche (1844–1900) believed that our purpose was to dominate and control the external forces that work on us, such as the Church and society. To be masters of our own destiny, he said, we had to develop inner mental strength.

LIFE UNTIL DEATH

Another German thinker, Martin Heidegger (1889–1976), looked at the meaning of what it is to be human. He said that we all try to make sense of our lives by engaging in various activities, whether work or play. But all along we're aware that there's a time limit on life—we're all going to die one day. It's only when we become aware of this that our life can start to have purpose or meaning.

WITH FREEDOM COMES RESPONSIBILITY

French existentialist Jean-Paul Sartre (1905–1980) said that, for humans, "existence precedes essence." In other words, it's only after we're born that we get to decide on our purpose. This, he said, makes us different from everything else in the world. Unlike a mug, broccoli, or a mouse, we have the freedom to shape ourselves and decide what we're going to become. To take advantage of this freedom, Sartre told us to break free of our normal ways of behaving, and to think carefully about how we want to act.

Remember, said Sartre, by making choices, we're setting an example for how a human life should be lived. If you decide to be an actor, a pilot, or a vet, you're saying that this is a good thing for people to be. In other words, this freedom we have is a big responsibility! We're not just responsible for the impact of our choices on ourselves and those around us, but also for their impact on the whole of humankind.

COLLISION COURSE

Like Sartre, Spanish philosopher José Ortega y Gasset (1883–1955) believed that we should constantly try to look at ourselves with fresh eyes and not get trapped in old habits of thinking. He said we can attempt to free ourselves from our current circumstances—where we live, what we do, our assumptions—by imagining new possibilities. The trouble was, the new possibilities would always clash with our current circumstances. That's why he described life as a series of collisions with the future.

Chocolate bar, your purpose is to be eaten!

Look out! For Ortega, life is a series of collisions with the future.

Sartre didn't believe in God or human nature. He said we make our own natures, so we have no excuses. But he still saw his message as positive because, as he put it:

"The destiny of man is placed within himself."

WHERE? WHEN?

WHAT ARE SPACE AND TIME?

Space and time are so much a part of our lives that we barely think about them. Yet, as we'll explore in this chapter, these concepts are not as straightforward as they first seem. They bring up big questions that theologians (people who study religion), philosophers, and scientists have wrestled with for centuries—questions that may never be fully answered.

IN THE BEGINNING

One question people ask is whether time and space have a beginning. Where and when did they start? According to Hindu teachings, the universe has no starting point, but goes through repeated cycles of creation, destruction, and rebirth. Ancient Greek philosophers believed the universe extends infinitely into the past.

Medieval Christian philosophers believed the universe began when God created it. But Augustine of Hippo (354–430 CE), an early Christian thinker, argued that, since God is eternal, he must exist outside of time. He saw no contradiction between this idea and his belief that the universe had a beginning. To the question, "What was God doing before the creation?" Augustine answered that, since God exists outside time, there is no "before the creation," so the question is meaningless.

DIVIDED OPINION

Another question philosophers ask is whether time and space exist outside of the human mind. Philosophers known as *realists*, including Plato, Aristotle, and Democritus, believed they do. Another set of thinkers called *idealists*, such as George Berkeley and Immanuel Kant, denied or doubted the external reality of space and time. In his *Critique of Pure Reason*, Kant described space and time as purely parts of a structure in our minds that allows us to understand the world. We need them, he

Is space simply a tool to measure the distance between things?

believed, to make sense of the information coming to us through our senses. So we measure space to see how big, or how far apart, objects are. And we measure time to see how long events take, or to work out the size of the gap between events. But this doesn't mean they exist on their own.

ONE AND THE SAME

Together, time and space make up the environment where we exist and through which we move. In that sense they're almost like two aspects of the same substance. In his *Theory of General Relativity* (1915), famous scientist Albert Einstein (see pages 56–57) showed how space and time are both part of a single entity, called *spacetime*.

Yet, when you look at space and time separately, they do seem very different. Time flows like a river, from the past to the future. Space doesn't travel anywhere. We can imagine empty space, but empty time, where nothing happens, is harder to imagine. Space is filled with objects, time with events. Objects can be moved and changed. Events, once they're in the past, can't be.

Time flows like a river, with a past and a future, a forward and a back.

"For any time, you can always imagine an earlier time." — Aristotle

EMPTY SPACE

CAN SPACE EXIST WITHOUT OBJECTS?

Imagine empty space. Think completely empty—no stars, no planets, not even a speck of dust, only blackness continuing forever. It's a bleak thought. But is it possible? Today, we know that it isn't. Einstein's Theory of General Relativity teaches us that even in deepest, darkest space, matter is still present in the form of subatomic particles, and there is also energy and gravity. But in the centuries prior to this discovery, many philosophers believed that empty space was perfectly possible.

NO OBJECT

English scientist Isaac Newton (1642–1726) believed that space is like an invisible box inside which objects exist and move. The objects don't affect the box, and they aren't affected by it. If you took away the objects, the box would still be there. The only difference between the universe and a box, said Newton, is that a box has defined dimensions, whereas the universe is infinite. This view of space as something that exists whether or not there are objects inside it is called *absolute space*.

German philosopher Gottfried Leibniz (1646–1716) didn't agree. He believed that space couldn't exist without the objects within it. Leibniz saw space as just a way of understanding the relationships between objects. So space enables us to say, for example, that there's an apple above Harry, a chair to the left, and a lawnmower to the right. To Leibniz, if there was only one object in the universe, space wouldn't exist, because there would be nothing to relate this object to. This view of space as something given meaning by the objects inside it is called *relative space*.

Relative space says that space exists in relation to objects.

FOOD FOR THOUGHT

Which universe is upside down?

To understand Leibniz's view of relative space, here's a thought experiment. Imagine two universes existing side by side. The only difference between them is that one of them is upside down. The thing is though, they can't agree which! The people of Universe A believe that they're the right way up and that Universe B is upside down, while the people of Universe B believe the opposite. The truth, Leibniz would say, is that both are right, and both are wrong. As there's no absolute space, there's no "right-way-up-ness" to compare themselves to—only each other. Therefore, no one can say which universe is upside down. All they can say is that they're both upside down relative to the other.

Newton came up with his own thought experiment to try to prove the existence of absolute space. Imagine, he said, a universe empty of everything except a bucket filled with water. If you were to set the bucket spinning, the water within would curve inward. This proves that the bucket and the water are moving (or else the water wouldn't form that shape). But moving relative to what? As there are no other objects in the universe, they must be moving relative to absolute space.

A change in the shape of the water shows that the bucket and water must be moving.

In the eighteenth century, Immanuel Kant came up with his own thought experiment to support the idea of an absolute universe. He gave the following example: Imagine a universe with nothing in it but a right-handed glove. If space was relative rather than absolute, he said, it would be impossible to tell whether the glove was right-handed.

EMPTY TIME

CAN TIME EXIST WITHOUT CHANGE?

What would happen if one day everything just stopped? Imagine it—at four o'clock one afternoon, the sun suddenly parks itself in the sky, the clouds become still, the sea turns to glass, and the hands on the clock stop turning. Not that we'd be aware of any of this, because we would be frozen in place, too! So, maybe this happens all the time. Who would know? If it did ever happen—and stuck—would that be the end of time?

Imagine if everything in the world froze—including you! Does time carry on?

TIME FOR CHANGE

Aristotle would say yes, time would also end at that point. He called time "the measure of change," and said, "There is no time apart from change." Gottfried Leibniz would agree with him (see pages 48–49). For Leibniz, time, like space, does not exist on its own. Time is just a way for us to understand the relationships between events. So time allows us to say, for example, that Rahul saw the cat before Harry broke the window, but after Maria went to Paris. Isaac Newton, on the other hand, would say that time continues whether or not there is change. So who is right?

FREEZING TIME

In 1969, the philosopher Sydney Shoemaker (born 1931) attempted to answer this question with the help of a thought experiment. Let's look at a simple version of this experiment. Imagine the whole universe is divided into two regions. We'll call them Five-Land and Eight-Land. There's no difference between them except that in Five-Land time freezes once every five years. Everything just stops for twelve months. For example, the Five-Landers went to bed on December 31 in Year 4, and they woke up on January 1 in Year 6. They weren't aware of losing this time, and they only found out about it because the Eight-Landers told them.

Similarly, in Eight-Land, time freezes once every eight years, and they only know about it because the Five-Landers tell them. The pattern goes on like this through the years, with the Five-Landers losing every fifth year, and the Eight-Landers losing every eighth year.

THE MYSTERY OF YEAR 40

All goes well until Year 40, when both regions freeze at the same time (because 40 is a multiple of both 8 and 5). Any change in the universe stops for twelve months, and then restarts at the beginning of Year 41.

The question is, can we really say time continued during Year 40, or that Year 40 even happened, if no one was there to witness it?

Shoemaker argues that time DID continue in that year, and that Year 40 DID happen. We know this because a pattern had been established that meant both regions would lose this year. The only difference between this and any other fifth or eighth year was that it happened to both groups at the same time. According to Shoemaker, this proves that time continues even when there's no change.

10 (or 11) today!

Do you agree? How would you feel about missing your birthday? Would you still be a year older?

OUR INNER CLOCK

HOW DO WE EXPERIENCE TIME?

Have you noticed how slowly the hands on the clock seem to move when you're in a classroom feeling hungry before lunch? But if you're watching a film or out having fun with your friends, time whizzes by? That's because *psychological time—* the way we experience time in our minds—is different from *clock time*. Clock time never varies. The length of seconds, minutes, and hours is always the same. It just seems to go faster or slower depending on our mood.

Early Christian philosopher St. Augustine wondered how we're able to describe the length of an event. What are we describing as "short" or "long"? It can't be what's in the past, as that no longer exists, and what doesn't exist has no properties. And it can't be the present, as the present has no duration.

He concluded that our experience of time is all in the mind.

SCARY MOMENTS

When something scary happens to you, how does time seem to move? Faster or slower than usual? You probably think it goes more slowly. But actually, of course it doesn't do either. It's only later, when you recall the scary moment, that you feel like it lasted for ages. That's a trick of memory. When you're scared, your senses are on high alert and you take in everything around you. With so many more memories of the event, it seems as though it lasted longer than it did.

Maria can sense time moving in the changing position of her dog.

IMAGINE THAT

We experience time every day in the changes we see around us. In the park, Maria watches her dog run over to the duck pond. She perceives the change in the dog's location as an event in time. Before, he was here, and now he's over there. Maria can also experience time with her eyes closed. She can remember the same dog as a puppy, running to the same pond yapping at the ducks. Her experience of these two events, separated by years, gives her a deeper impression of time, and how it can mean changes over a longer period. Keeping her eyes closed, Maria can also imagine a time in the future when her dog is old and no longer able to run so fast. Many philosophers believe that our ability to experience and imagine other times is a big part of what makes us conscious thinkers.

NOW AND THEN

Jamila is eating an apple, concentrating on its crunchiness and sweetness. She's determined not to think about anything else. She's not thinking about her day at school or what song she's going to play later—just the apple! She wants to experience "now" as fully as she can. She takes another bite. Crunch! Yum! But what exactly is this "now"? Is it a tiny instant of time or does it last a few seconds? Brain scientists have measured what we call "now" and found that it lasts around 80 milliseconds. They've also found out that we don't actually live in the present, but very slightly in the past. That's because our brains take time to reconstruct a story of what's happening based on the information coming from our senses. Bad luck, Jamila!

53

DOES TIME EXIST?

IS TIME WHAT IT SEEMS TO BE?

We can see a clock, but we can't see "time." So how do we know time is real? The answer might seem pretty obvious—time must exist, or else what are clocks measuring? But maybe, a skeptic could reply, they're not measuring anything! You could invent a device for measuring the length of a unicorn's horn, but that doesn't mean unicorns are real.

BEYOND US

Is it possible that time is just something we've invented in order to measure the changes we see around us? Parmenides thought that change was an illusion (see pages 34–35), so maybe time is too. It could simply be the way our minds perceive reality. British scientist Arthur Eddington (1882–1944) believed that chairs and tables look the way they do because we can't see what they really are, which is an arrangement of atoms. Time could be the same. It might be something completely different! Just as bees and butterflies can see shades we can't, and bats and dolphins can hear sounds beyond the range of our hearing, maybe human brains can't comprehend what time really is (see pages 60–61 for a theory on what time might actually be).

But even if we found out that time was something else, would that make it any less real? When scientists discovered that heat was caused by the motion of molecules, and not by the action of a mysterious fluid as they originally believed, it didn't mean that heat stopped being real. You could still boil an egg with

it. And just because we don't know what time is, it doesn't mean we don't need it. For one thing, it helps us know when that egg is ready to be eaten!

CLOCK CURRENCY

Unlike devices that measure unicorn horns, clocks exist because we need them. In that sense, clocks are a bit like money. They're both things that were invented to measure something important to us. Clocks measure motion and change, while money measures value. Before money was invented, people would barter. They might swap some eggs for a sack of corn, or a box of apples for a haircut. This caused problems because the apple grower might not want a haircut. So money was invented as a standard measure against which all goods and services could be valued.

Trade didn't start when money was invented— it's just that money made trade a lot easier. In the same way, time didn't start when clocks were invented. Before clocks, people knew the rough time by checking the position of the sun in the sky. All clocks did was make the measuring of time a lot easier and more accurate.

In the past, people used the sun to help tell time.

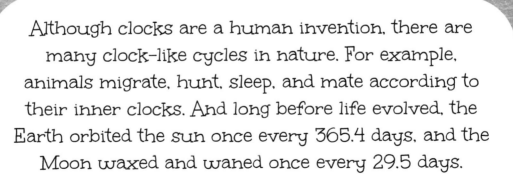

Although clocks are a human invention, there are many clock-like cycles in nature. For example, animals migrate, hunt, sleep, and mate according to their inner clocks. And long before life evolved, the Earth orbited the sun once every 365.4 days, and the Moon waxed and waned once every 29.5 days.

No one was around to measure these things, but they still happened with perfect regularity, and they will continue to happen long after we're gone.

THEORIES IN TIME: ALBERT EINSTEIN

Albert Einstein was probably the greatest scientist of the twentieth century. His theories have had enormous implications for philosophy and our understanding of the nature of time. Einstein was born in Germany, but went to school in Switzerland. After graduating, he got a job in a patent office. He moved back to Germany in 1914 and became the director of a school. As a Jewish man, Einstein faced threats to his life when the Nazis came to power in 1933, and he moved to Princeton, New Jersey, where he taught physics for the remainder of his life.

SORRY, NEWTON

In 1905, while working in the patent office, Einstein came up with his *Special Theory of Relativity*. He proposed that the speed at which light travels in empty space (186,000 miles per second) is constant (it never varies), and that this had remarkable consequences for our understanding of time.

He realized, for one thing, that you cannot say an event happened at exactly the same time for different observers. For example, imagine Maria is in a spaceship orbiting Saturn, while Rahul is in an observatory on Earth. If Maria sees a comet hitting Saturn, Rahul will see the same event 70 minutes later. That's because it takes 70 minutes for the light from Saturn to reach Earth.

Einstein's discovery was a major blow to Isaac Newton's theory that there is a universal clock keeping the same time throughout the universe.

IT'S ALL RELATIVE

Einstein's Special Theory of Relativity also showed something else—the way we experience time depends on our motion through space.

Imagine Harry is a passenger standing in the middle of a fast train. Jamila is standing in a field next to the track, watching Harry's train go by. Suddenly, lightning strikes both ends of the train. Jamila sees the two lightning bolts strike at the same time. Harry, though, is moving toward the bolt at the front of the train. So he sees the flash from the front bolt slightly before the flash from the rear bolt because the light from the front of the train has a shorter distance to travel to get to him.

But how is that possible, when the strikes occurred at the same time? Einstein explained that Jamila and Harry experienced time differently. Time must have slowed down for Harry. Einstein realized from this that the faster we travel through space, the slower time moves for us.

Later, with his *General Theory of Relativity* (1915), Einstein showed that time goes slower for people when they are close to a massive body, such as a planet, due to the effect of gravity. So time actually

moves faster in space than it does on Earth. Time, therefore, is relative—how we experience it depends on where we are and how fast we're moving.

"Time and space are modes by which we think, and not conditions in which we live." — Albert Einstein

BEFORE THE BIG BANG

DID TIME ALWAYS EXIST, AND WILL IT GO ON EXISTING?

How big is the past, and how big is the future? Philosophers have asked these questions since ancient times, and in the twentieth century, science began to answer them. American astronomer Edwin Hubble discovered, in 1929, that the universe is expanding. This led scientists to conclude that the universe began with a "big bang," when a tiny point of incredible heat and density exploded outward to create the cosmos of today. They calculated that this happened around 13.7 billion years ago.

SIZING UP THE PAST

But this leads to another question—what happened before the big bang? Scientists answer that time, as well as space, was created by the big bang, so asking what happened before it makes no sense. As British physicist Stephen Hawking said, it's like asking what's north of the North Pole. If the big bang theory is true, it answers the question about the size of the past—it's 13.7 billion years.

Is there anything north of the North Pole?

THE BIG BOUNCE

However, many scientists and philosophers are bothered by the idea of the big bang as being something that just happened without any cause. Everything else in the universe has a cause, they say, so why not the big bang?

Another theory offers a way out of this paradox—it's known as "the big bounce." This theory proposes that the big bang was caused by a previous universe that shrunk down to a dense point (known as the "big crunch"), and then exploded outward in a big bang.

According to the big bounce theory, our universe will one day also start to shrink. In fact, this cycle of shrinking and expanding might have been going on forever and might never stop. Some scientists have even suggested that time could run backward during the shrinking phase.

THE BIG CHILL

The big bounce theory is similar to Hindu teachings about a cyclical universe (see page 46). But could it be true? It seems unlikely, according to current research. Astronomers have discovered that the expansion of the universe is actually getting FASTER. Gravitational forces do not seem to be strong enough to cause this expansion to stop.

This could mean a somewhat bleaker future for the universe—rather than a big bounce, we're heading for a "big chill." The universe will continue to expand, with the stars and galaxies spreading farther and farther apart. As the universe gets colder, all life will eventually disappear. Even the last stars will burn out, and there will be nothing left but cold, empty space. That is a very long time away though!

So it seems that the universe has a finite past and an infinite future.

But once all lifeforms have vanished, can we still call what happens next the future? Whose future would it be?

NO TIME LIKE THE PRESENT

I'M SAFE ... BECAUSE THE FUTURE DOESN'T EXIST!

DO THE FUTURE AND THE PAST EXIST?

It seems obvious to us that the present moment exists, and so does everything in it. The book you're reading, for example, exists. But what about things in the past and the future? It sounds wrong to say that dinosaurs exist, or that next week's news exists. The word exists implies "exists now." In the way we experience the flow of time, the past is the part of our lives that has slipped out of existence, while the future is the part that has yet to exist.

THE PROBLEM WITH PRESENTISM

The belief that only the present moment exists is called *presentism*. It seems, at first glance, a very common-sense sort of belief. But there are problems with it.

For example, how can we say the present moment exists when it's constantly changing? And if only the present exists, why do we spend so much time thinking about the past and planning for the future? They seem to exist in our minds at least—and not only there! We can even see the past in photographs.

But the biggest argument against presentism is Einstein's Special Theory of Relativity (see pages 56–57). This shows that there isn't just one present moment that we all share. People separated by large distances experience different presents. We can't all point to one present moment and say "that exists." In fact, the present can be as slippery as the past and the future.

LAYERS UPON LAYERS

Other rival theories have come along to challenge presentism. One of these is *possibilism*. This says that the past and present both exist, but the future doesn't. Possibilists imagine the past as a block that's gradually growing upward. The present is the topmost layer, which is being added to all the time. As each new layer of present is added, the former present becomes part of the past. Possibilism emphasizes that there's a difference between the past, which is fixed, and the future, which is not formed.

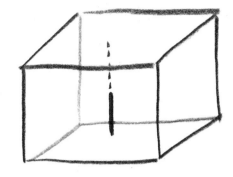

Eternalists say that the universe is an already complete block.

A FIXED FUTURE

The other rival theory of time is *eternalism*. Eternalists believe that the past, present, and future are all equally real. The universe isn't a growing block, but a complete one. Time is one dimension on this block, and it's just as solid as the three dimensions of space. Eternalists believe that our view of time as something that flows from past to future is an illusion. It's just the way our brains perceive reality. In fact, they say, the future is as fixed as the past. Many philosophers are uncomfortable with this idea, because it suggests that we have no free will. If the future is fixed, then we have no power to change things with our actions.

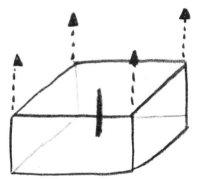

In possibilism, the present is constantly being added in layers on top of a fixed past.

Let's take the example of a headache. If a headache exists, it hurts. It can't exist and not hurt. So it exists in the present.

Past and future headaches don't hurt, so in that sense they don't exist in the same way. Yet they do influence the way we behave—if you know from past experience that stress gives you headaches, you'll try to avoid stress to prevent future pain. **So headaches exist in memory in the past and in potential in the future.**

TIME TRAVEL

CAN WE TRAVEL TO THE PAST OR THE FUTURE?

In fact, we all travel through time—we're heading into the future right now, at a rate of one second per second. But it doesn't feel like time travel because we're all doing it together. Usually, when people talk about time travel, they mean when someone's personal time gets out of step with everyone else's. This might involve travel to the future, or travel to the past. Travel to the past especially has been the subject of much discussion by philosophers.

THINKING THE IMPOSSIBLE

Many thinkers believe that it's not possible to travel to the past. If you went back in time, they say, you might meet your younger self. There would be two of you existing at the same time, and that's impossible! You could also die before you were born, which seems even more unimaginable.

Travel to the past also causes problems for cause-and-effect, the principle that everything that happens has a past cause. In this case, your arrival in the past actually had a future cause—your decision to travel there.

Is it possible to meet another version of yourself?

WHO'S YOUR DADDY?

The most famous problem connected with travel to the past is the "grandfather paradox." Let's say a young man named Peter goes back in time and kills his grandfather when his grandfather is young. This means that Peter's grandfather would never grow up to be the father of the girl who would become Peter's mother. If Peter's mother never existed, then Peter didn't either, so who went back in time to kill Peter's grandfather?

ENDLESS LOOPS

And there's another problem. Imagine that one October 1st, Maria travels one month back in time. Time goes by, and October 1st arrives once more. Maria has no choice but to travel back to September 1st again. Her appearance in the past has forced this future decision to be made. Does this mean that Maria has no freedom to change her mind? That seems unlikely.

Let's further imagine that on September 15th, Jamila writes an essay that wins a prize. When October 1st comes and it's time for Maria to step back into her time machine, she takes Jamila's essay with her. On September 1st, Maria hands it to Jamila. At this stage, Jamila hasn't yet written the essay. She decides to copy the essay Maria gave her, and she wins the prize. The following month Maria again travels back and gives Jamila the essay. This loop in time may have been going on forever. So who wrote the original essay?

WHAT'S IT GOING TO BE?

Because of these various problems and paradoxes, many philosophers believe that backward time travel is simply impossible. Others say that it might be possible, but you couldn't change the past in any way. Something would prevent Peter from killing his grandfather, or Maria from giving Jamila a copy of her essay.

On June 28, 2009, British physicist Stephen Hawking threw a party for time travelers. Invitations were sent out only AFTER the party was over. "I sat there a long time," he reported, "but no one came."

WORLD WITHOUT END

WHAT IS INFINITY?

We live in a world of things that can be measured. You can measure the length of your desk, the weight of your phone, or the time it takes you to walk to school. Simple, right? But then there's another kind of quantity—the infinite (the things you can't measure), and that's where it all goes a bit wild.

TO INFINITY

We can look up at the night sky and imagine that space goes on without end. We can count: 1, 2, 3, 4, and then just keep going forever. This kind of infinity is easy enough to understand, even if it does boggle our minds. What's trickier is the idea that ordinary objects or distances might also be infinite, when looked at another way.

SLOW AND STEADY

We can thank the ancient Greek philosopher Zeno of Elea for introducing us to this idea of infinity. He asked us to imagine a race between legendary Greek hero Achilles, and a tortoise. To give the tortoise a chance, the race officials give it a head start. Even so, it seems like a no-brainer that speedy Achilles will win the race. The race begins and Achilles immediately starts closing in on the tortoise. But by the time he's closed the gap, the tortoise has moved on a little farther, creating a new gap. The new gap is smaller, but it's still a finite distance that Achilles must cover to catch up with the tortoise. Achilles races across the new gap, but to his frustration, the tortoise has by now established yet another gap. This continues to happen, with the gap between them getting ever smaller, but never quite disappearing. The result is that Achilles can never catch up with the tortoise.

PARADOX UPON PARADOX

Zeno's story of Achilles and the tortoise is a paradox, because it's obviously wrong, but it's hard for us to explain why. The problem is that he's introduced the idea of infinity into something we regard as finite, like the gap between Achilles and the tortoise. He's done this by breaking up this distance into an infinite number of smaller distances that Achilles needs to cross.

Is it really an infinite number? If we keep dividing the distance, maybe we'll eventually come to a distance so small that it can't be divided up any further. If so, this would simply lead to another paradox—a distance that small would have no length at all, because if it had a length it could always be divided further. But how can the space that Achilles must cover be made up of no length?

We know that in the real world Achilles will always catch up with (and overtake) the tortoise. Put another way, you could divide up your walk to school into infinitely small periods of time—but that doesn't mean you won't get there!

If you're confused, don't worry. Infinity can be extremely strange, and mathematicians have spent many years trying to explain this paradox!

Is the distance of your walk to school finite or infinite?

"It is always possible to think of a larger number, for the number of times a distance can be bisected [divided in half] is infinite. Hence the infinite is potential, never actual." — Aristotle

MIND AND BODY

IS YOUR MIND DIFFERENT FROM YOUR BODY?

You might feel that your mind and body are separate, but thoughts can cause physical changes in your body. For example, what's the most delicious meal you can imagine? Think about it for a few seconds. Is your mouth watering? This is an example of how a thought can cause physical changes in your body. Feelings can do the same thing. For example, if you're scared, you might feel a knot in your stomach.

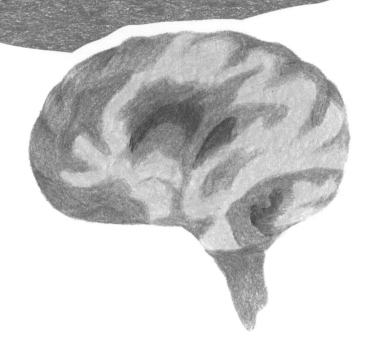

MIND AND MATTER

It's strange though, isn't it? Thoughts and feelings don't seem to be physical, so how can they have physical effects? This leads us to ask what exactly thoughts are. Most people believe thoughts arise in the mind. In that case, what's the mind? Is it the same thing as the brain? If not, then what and where is it?

Some people believe that although the mind controls the body, it's actually not a part of the body at all. The idea of the body and mind being separate is known as *dualism*. French philosopher René Descartes believed that the human body is made of matter, like a rock or a tree, and can't think for itself. The human mind, he argued, does the thinking, but it doesn't have a physical form. It doesn't take up space and isn't controlled by physical laws.

ANOTHER VIEW

The problem with Descartes' dualism is this—if the mind and the body are separate, how do they interact? How does your mind tell your body to walk, if it has no physical form? And if you trip and fall, how does this physical event cause your mind to feel pain? Descartes couldn't explain this, but he thought it might happen in the brain's pineal gland.

On the other side of the debate was the thinker Thomas Hobbes. Hobbes was a *materialist*, who saw both the mind and the body as part of the material world. He believed that Descartes had confused the thinking thing (the brain) with the action of thinking. We wouldn't say breathing is something in itself, but is an action performed by our lungs. In the same way, the mind (our thoughts, ideas, and perceptions) isn't a thing, but an action performed by the brain.

When you think and feel, are your brain and mind one and the same?

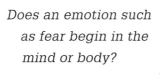

Does an emotion such as fear begin in the mind or body?

SIDE EFFECTS

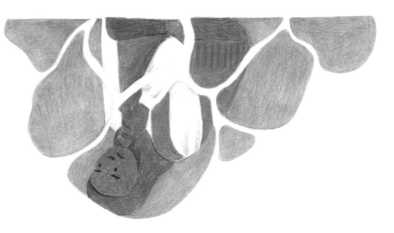

The scientist Thomas Henry Huxley believed that thoughts and feelings are caused by physical sensations in the body, but can't affect it. Let's look at an example. You see a scary picture, which causes your heart to beat faster, and goosebumps to rise on your skin. These physical changes *bring on* a feeling of fear. In other words, fear isn't the cause of bodily change, just a side effect of that change.

What do you think?

Are your mind and body the same thing, or is there something else going on?

CAUSING CONTROVERSY: BARUCH SPINOZA

Baruch Spinoza was born into a Jewish family in Amsterdam. He was a modest, hard-working man, who made a living as a philosophy teacher and lens grinder. He tried to lead a moral life, but he often got into trouble with religious authorities because of his views. At the age of 23, he was thrown out of his Jewish synagogue in Amsterdam. Then, 19 years later, he was condemned as an atheist (a non-believer) by Christians, and his books were publicly set on fire.

ONE FOR ALL

So what were these dangerous views? Spinoza wasn't actually an atheist—he did believe in God—but his views on the nature of God were different from those of other people at the time. Spinoza, a bit like Parmenides, believed that everything in the universe is one. "There is only one substance," he declared, "and that substance we can conceive of as either Nature or God." This substance, he said, has an infinite number of properties, but we can only perceive two of them—matter and thought. Spinoza saw mind and body as different aspects of the same divine substance, like two sides of the same coin.

In this way, Spinoza managed to avoid the difficulties faced by Descartes (see pages 66–67), who saw mind and body as separate. To Spinoza, when something happens in the body, it also happens in the mind, and vice versa, because both are different forms of the same substance.

TROUBLE BREWING

Spinoza believed that everything in the universe is part of this divine substance, and everything that happens is necessary. This is where Spinoza got into trouble with the Christians. He saw "evil" as part of this same substance. But Spinoza believed that the concept of evil is actually an illusion. We see something as evil because we can't see the bigger picture or the chain of cause-and-effect that makes it all part of God's reality.

Even free will is an illusion, according to Spinoza. We believe we're free because we're aware of making decisions, but we're unaware of the causes of those decisions. The decisions come from appetites and emotions within our bodies, which are a necessary expression of the divine reality. (For more on free will, see pages 82–83.)

THINGS THAT THINK

Spinoza believed that all objects have mental as well as physical aspects. This includes not just humans and animals, but also tables, rivers, and carrots. He made clear that such objects would have very simple mental states, and not what we would call "minds." Many people have had trouble accepting this part of Spinoza's theories.

What does a table think about?

According to Spinoza, the mind and body are two sides of the same coin.

> "Mind and body are one."
> — Baruch Spinoza

I FEEL FOR YOU

CAN ANYONE EVER REALLY KNOW HOW ANOTHER PERSON FEELS?

Harry's been punished by his dad for breaking a window. He's not allowed to go out to see a movie this evening. Maria tries to cheer him up. "I know how you feel," she says. Harry turns on her: "I've been looking forward to this movie for weeks. You can't possibly know how I feel!" Is Harry right? Is it really impossible for a person to know how someone else is feeling? It's true that emotions are private things that only the person feeling them can experience. But does that mean we're completely closed off from each other?

RIGHT AND WRONG

Even if Maria doesn't know how much this movie means to Harry, she can understand how he feels in a more general way. We all share certain general emotions, including frustration, excitement, joy, and sadness. Harry is sad. Maria sometimes feels sad, too. By imagining what Harry is going through in a general way, she is *empathizing* with him.

There's another problem with Harry's statement. Can you spot the paradox? If Harry's saying that Maria can't know how he feels, it follows that HE can't know how SHE feels either. Therefore, he can't say that she doesn't know how he feels. So if Harry's right, he's also wrong! This is known as the "paradox of empathy."

FEELING LIKE A FISH

A tale from ancient China expresses this paradox very well. Philosopher Zhuang Zhou is standing on a bridge with his friend Hui Shi, watching the fish swim by. Zhuang Zhou remarks, "The fish are happy." Hui Shi replies, "You aren't a fish. How do you know the fish are happy?" To which Zhuang Zhou responds: "You aren't me, so how do you know that I don't know the fish are happy?" Hui Shi accepts this, but still points out that Zhuang Zhou isn't a fish, which is why he finds it hard to believe his claim.

Hui Shi makes a good point. Even with empathy, we'd probably struggle to understand how fish or other animals feel. But could science help? If we were to really study an animal, such as a bat, couldn't we discover how it feels to be that animal? Philosopher Thomas Nagel (born 1937) explored this question in his famous 1974 essay "What is it Like to Be a

Can we know how a bat feels?

Bat?" He argued that we might be able to imagine what it's like to fly, navigate by sonar, hang upside down, and eat insects, but we'd still never be able to FEEL like a bat. Private thoughts and feelings, Nagel said, are the only things that are unique to each individual, whether human or animal, so only an individual can know what it's like to be itself.

"Though our brother is upon the rack, as long as we ourselves are at our ease, our senses will never inform us of what he suffers. They never did, and never can, carry us beyond our own person, and it is by the imagination only that we can form any conception of what are his sensations."
— David Hume

OTHER MINDS

HOW DO I KNOW THAT YOU HAVE A MIND?

When she was younger, Jamila often had the feeling that she was the only person in the world who had a mind. She strongly suspected that everyone else was actually a robot. They might look and sound like real people, but they were all just machines inside, with no thoughts and feelings of their own. Even now, when someone does something odd or unexpected, she thinks to herself, *Oh no! One of the robots has malfunctioned!* Could Jamila be right? Is there any way of being sure?

DUCKS IN A ROW

Philosophers call this "the problem of other minds." The thinker John Stuart Mill (1806–1873) believed that other people did have minds, because their bodies and ways of behaving were similar to his own, and they used language just like he did. This gave him strong reasons to believe they had thoughts and feelings like he did.

Another way of expressing Mill's argument would be—if it looks like a duck, swims like a duck, and quacks like a duck, then it's probably a duck!

Does everyone else have a mind?
Or could everyone except you be a robot?

FAKING IT

Jamila doesn't think much of Mill's reasoning. She points out that Robot Rahul could just be pretending to be human. He could fake a toothache, for example, by groaning and clutching his jaw, but that doesn't prove to her that he actually has a toothache.

Even if we assume the other person has a mind, it doesn't mean that what he calls a toothache is the same as what I call a toothache. We learn these terms through conversation with other people, but we can never be sure that we're all talking about the same thing.

"[O]n the one hand I have a clear and distinct idea of myself, in so far as I am simply a thinking, non-extended thing [that is, a mind], and on the other hand I have a distinct idea of body, in so far as this is simply an extended, non-thinking thing. And accordingly, it is certain that I am really distinct from my body, and can exist without it." – René Descartes

NO BRAINER

Another approach to this question of other minds is to look at how the mind relates to the body (see pages 66–67). If the mind is a product of the brain's activity, as some philosophers believe, then that would suggest that other people have minds too. After all, their brains are the same as Jamila's, so why should only her brain produce a mind and not theirs? Or if, as Thomas Hobbes believed, consciousness is simply the operation of the brain itself, then it follows that we must all have minds, since we all have brains.

On the other hand, if the mind and body are separate, as dualists like René Descartes argue, it becomes much harder to prove Jamila wrong. No one can tell her for sure that other people have minds, even if all their brains function just the same as hers.

In the end, the thing that's finally convinced Jamila that other people do have minds is reading poetry and listening to music. It may not be the sort of proof that would convince a philosopher, but for Jamila it seems impossible that such beautiful works could be created by mindless robots.

ARTIFICIAL INTELLIGENCE

CAN A MACHINE THINK?

Machines are all around us—clocks, toasters, hairdryers, lawnmowers. They all do useful things, but none of them can be said to "think." What about more advanced machines, such as computers and robots? When you ask your phone to tell you the day's weather, does it think before it replies?

WHAT IS "THINKING"?

To answer these questions, we first need to decide what we mean by "think." Thinking, in the human sense, can mean learning, problem-solving, reasoning, calculating, and deciding. Sophisticated machines can do all these things. They use these skills to help doctors identify diseases, understand and respond to human speech, and even beat you at chess! But is that all there is to human thinking? What about self-awareness—being conscious of yourself as an individual? When a computer is performing its clever calculations, is it actually aware of anything?

TEST THE MACHINE

In 1950, British computer pioneer Alan Turing (1912–1954) proposed a test for machine intelligence. He suggested that a human should interview a machine and another human without knowing which was which. The test should be repeated several times. If the interviewer believed the machine was human in more than half of the tests, then the machine could be said to be intelligent. In 2014, a computer program called Eugene Goostman became the first machine to pass the Turing Test. The result was later criticized because "Eugene" was posing as a 13-year-old Ukrainian boy with poor English, which made the conversation quite limited.

PROGRAMMED TO SUCCEED

Other machines may pass the Turing Test in the future, but even so, is this really proof that machines can think? American philosopher John Searle (born 1932) doesn't believe so. He offered a thought experiment known as the "Chinese Room" to explain why. Searle asked us to imagine him in a closed room. Imagine that he receives questions in Chinese through a slot in the door. He doesn't understand Chinese, but he has a set of English instructions to help him process the Chinese symbols. He chooses the right responses to send back through the slot using these instructions.

Searle is saying that he's like a computer in this scenario—like him, a computer doesn't actually understand Chinese, it's simply following a program.

The difference between us and machines is that when we answer a question, we understand the answer we give. And of course we have the internal awareness that we call consciousness. This doesn't just allow us to think, but also to laugh, cry, hate, and love. Machines are a long way from being able to do any of that!

It's fascinating to imagine that one day scientists might be able to build a machine that can think and feel just like us.

But would this invention also be a sad thing? Would it mean that we're all basically flesh-and-blood robots, and our brains are just very sophisticated computers?

WHO ARE WE REALLY?

WHAT GIVES US OUR IDENTITY?

Oliver is boarding a telepod to Mars. Anne is worried. "Are you sure you don't want to take the rocket?" she asks. "And waste months in space when I can be there in seconds? No way," replies Oliver. "See you when I get back!" The telepod scans Oliver's brain and body cell by cell and beams the information to Mars, where he is reassembled. His original body is discarded in the process.

COPIES OF COPIES

After two fun weeks on Mars, Oliver beams himself back to Earth. "What a fantastic trip!" he says to Anne, as he climbs out of the telepod. She looks at him closely. He's now a copy of a copy of the Oliver she said goodbye to, but he seems no different. "Are you sure you're all right?" she asks. "Fine!" laughs Oliver. "You should come with me next time."

What is it that makes Oliver "Oliver"? Does it matter that every part of his physical body and brain has been replaced by a copy? It doesn't seem to bother him. He feels the same inside, after all. Surely all that matters is that his consciousness has carried on surviving.

This isn't just a science fiction question. According to scientists, the human body replaces itself with a completely new set of cells roughly every seven to ten years. So what the telepod does to the body in seconds is happening to us anyway—just much more slowly!

Oliver's body is disassembled and reassembled when he travels by telepod. Is he still the same person?

So who are we? Our minds, our bodies, or both?

STATE OF MIND

What if the telepod didn't copy Oliver properly, and instead put him back together as a giant fly on Mars? So long as he continued to think of himself as Oliver, most people would agree that that's who he was. The Bohemian writer Franz Kafka (1883–1924) wrote a story called "Metamorphosis" about a man named Gregor who woke up in the body of a giant beetle. We accept that Gregor is the beetle because his mind is still there inside it, telling us what it feels like to be a beetle. So it seems to be our minds that make us who we are, not our bodies.

If Oliver loses his memory, can he still be Oliver?

REMEMBER ME

But let's say the telepod made a different sort of copying error ... Imagine that the reassembled version of Oliver looked like Oliver but had no MEMORIES of being Oliver. Imagine his entire past had been wiped from his mind. Would you then say that the original Oliver was now dead? If that was the case, then what about people who lose their memories after an accident? Would you say that they had died, too? Their family and friends would almost certainly disagree!

SELF-SEEKING

IS THERE SUCH A THING AS THE SELF?

Imagine floating in darkness. You can't see, hear, smell, taste, or touch anything—not even your own body. You have no memories. It's as if you've just popped into existence out of nowhere. This is the "flying man" thought experiment created by Islamic philosopher Avicenna (980–1037). In such a situation, would your mind be blank? Avicenna thought not. He believed that even in this state you'd be aware of your own existence. In other words, you'd still have a sense of your own self.

Could our sense of "me" be just a chain of linked perceptions?

MISSING LINK

But is the self a real thing? On pages 76–77, we learned that our bodies change over time—all our cells are gradually replaced. At the same time, our attitudes, beliefs, and personalities develop as we experience more of life. Yet through all this change, we still feel like we're the same person. Inside, we're always ourselves, no matter how much we change. Could that be an illusion? David Hume thought so (see pages 26–27). He believed the thing we call "me" is just a series of perceptions linked together like a chain.

YESTERDAY'S NEWS

But if the self is an illusion and we're nothing more than a series of linked experiences, this could cause problems. Imagine this situation: Harry has to go to football training early tomorrow morning, so he asks Rahul to wake him up. "I can be pretty rude in the mornings," warns Harry, "but please don't take no for an answer."

The next morning Rahul wakes Harry. "Go away!" groans Harry, rolling over and going back to sleep. What does Rahul do? If there's no permanent self inside Harry and he's just a series of experiences, Rahul should do what Harry is saying now and go away. But if Rahul believes that Harry has a self that persists through time—if he's sure that the Harry of today is the same as the Harry of yesterday—then he should take the advice of yesterday's Harry and keep trying to wake him.

In a more serious case, imagine a burglar saying that he's no longer the same person who broke into a house last week and stole some money. There are very good reasons why, in society, we need to believe that the self is real. If we thought otherwise, then no one would ever need to take responsibility for their actions.

GO AWAY!

Writer and psychologist Susan Blackmore (born 1951) believes the self is like a story we make up about ourselves. We experience life as a stream of information coming to us through our senses like dots on a page. Every now and then we join the dots and say, "That's me!" But it's only an invention.

Blackmore says: "This so-called me is really just another reconstruction. There was an earlier one 30 minutes ago, and there will be others in the future. But they're really not the same person."

LANGUAGE AND THE MIND

CAN WE THINK WITHOUT LANGUAGE?

Think about something you enjoy doing. What's in your head when you think about it? Whatever it is, it's probably not words. When you feel happy, you don't say to yourself, "I feel happy." We don't need language to experience emotion. It's the same with perception. When you see something red, you don't normally think of the word "red." When we listen to music, paint a picture, or do mathematics, we don't use words much at all. Language doesn't really play a role in this kind of thinking.

WORD PLAY

It's when your thinking becomes more complicated that words start to get involved. For example, Rahul decides he wants to buy a new jacket. He thinks about his desire to "buy a new jacket" and he might go on to think that "there's one in a new store in town."

Language helps us organize our thoughts, form ideas, and reflect on them. British-American philosopher Peter Carruthers (born 1952) argues that we have a kind of inner language that allows us to bring our thoughts into conscious awareness. When early humans developed language, it enabled them to name and think about abstract concepts such as beauty, art, love, and war.

How do you think? What's in your mind when you do?

LIMITED TO LANGUAGE

Particular languages may affect the way their speakers think about things. For example, in English we have just one word for camel, whereas there are more than forty words for this animal in Arabic. As a result, an English speaker's thoughts on camels may be fairly limited compared to an Arabic speaker's. Interestingly, the ancient Greeks and Romans had no word for blue. And the English had no word for orange until the word appeared in 1512. Is it possible that the appearance of words for these shades affected the way people thought about them?

How would you think about orange and blue if there were no words for them?

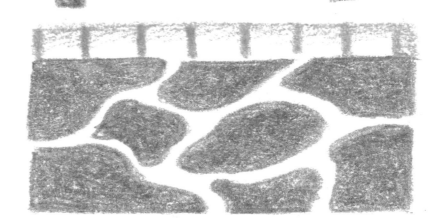

NO WORDS

What happens to children who are never exposed to language? Are they able to think?

In American Sign Language teacher Susan Schaller's book, *A Man Without Words* (1991), Schaller describes the case of a deaf man named Ildefonso who lived in complete isolation and never learned any language. Once she had taught him sign language, he told Schaller that he grew up with no concept of time and without knowing that people and things even had names.

Nevertheless, Schaller found evidence that he had been able to think and reason without language. He had formed memories and went on to communicate them later, when he was able to do so.

"We may be able to think without language, but language lets us know that we are thinking."
— Arika Okrent, linguist

FREE WILL

ARE WE FREE TO MAKE OUR OWN CHOICES?

Try this—raise your hand and scratch your ear. Now do another action—whatever you like. It's your choice this time! Did you do it? It seems like we have free will, doesn't it? You just performed an action that was entirely your own choice. (Or maybe you ignored the request completely, and that was your choice, too!) But are we really free to act as we choose? Philosophers have debated this question since ancient times. Some say that the future is determined (fixed) and that free will is an illusion, while others take the opposite view.

CHOOSING TO CHANGE

Aristotle believed in free will. He admitted that many of the things we do are determined by our habits and character, but we're always free to change these if we want.

Christian philosophers such as Augustine and Thomas Aquinas believed that God is outside of time and therefore knows all our future actions, but the CHOICES we make are still our own. So in the Bible story, Adam and Eve were free to choose whether or not to eat the apple, AND God knew what choice they would make. But if God made Adam and Eve, including their characters, and he knew what they were going to choose, can we really call it free will? And was it fair of him to punish them?

OUT OF CHARACTER

David Hume believed that the future is determined, but we do still have free will. This seems, at first glance, like a paradox. What he meant was that everything we choose to do is determined by our CHARACTER. Our feelings and passions govern our actions.

German philosopher Arthur Schopenhauer (1788–1860) put it well when he said: "Man can do what he wills but he cannot will what he wills." In other words, we can ACT on our desires, but we can't CHANGE our desires.

Jamila wants to prove Hume and Schopenhauer wrong. She decides to paint her door pink, even though she HATES pink. She wants to show she has free will and is not a slave to her passions!

BRAIN POWER

René Descartes said that the physical body isn't free, but the mind is. However, today's brain scientists seem to have proved the opposite—they've discovered that the brain makes decisions half a second or more before we're aware of it! So if you think of your consciousness as "you," that could mean you don't have free will. On the other hand, if "you" includes your body, then it's you who's making the decision, even if it doesn't sound exactly like free will!

IT IS MY DECISION TO TAKE THE DOG FOR A WALK.

Immanuel Kant believed we can't know for sure whether we have free will, but **we must act as if we have it.**

We should use our powers of reason to think deeply about our actions and their consequences, and then try to make moral choices. If we didn't do this, he said, it would be wrong to hold people responsible for their actions.

DOUBLE TROUBLE

WHAT IF "I" BECAME "WE"?

Oliver is walking down the street one day when he bumps into himself. Shock quickly turns to anger as each Oliver accuses the other of being an imposter. But the more they question each other, the more they realize how identical they are in every way. Not only do they look the same, but they also share the same personality, interests, desires, and memories.

MISTAKEN IDENTITY

From that day forward, life gets very confusing for Oliver—or make that the Olivers! "He" has become "they," and this causes big trouble at home and at school. Their family, friends, and teachers don't know who the real Oliver is. Is it one of them, both, or neither?

The case of the Olivers makes us think more carefully about personal identity and what it is. We're used to thinking that identity is housed within an individual person, and is not something that can be shared or split. The word individual literally means "not divisible."

According to British philosopher Derek Parfit (1942–2017), identity can change. It's always developing. The moment Oliver became two people, so did his identity. Oliver 1 will go off and have his own experiences and develop new memories. Oliver 2 will do the same. Before long they will become different people with their own separate identities.

Who is the real Oliver?

MAKING MEMORIES

Parfit acknowledged that individuals are made up of brains and bodies, but he felt identity was more than that. It's also our memories and what he called our "souls" that make us who we are. Is that right? How important is memory to your identity?

Let's imagine a future technology that allows Maria to upload her memories to Jamila's mind. Instead of showing her photos of a trip to Paris, Maria just sends Jamila her memories. Gradually, Jamila forgets that these aren't her memories. She starts to remember Paris as if she went there herself. Soon it's not just travel memories the two friends share. It's almost as if they've shared the same past. You can see how this could cause some blurring of identities!

YOU DO YOU

The other part of identity that Parfit mentioned was "soul," which could also be described as "selfhood." This is tricky to define.

To give an example, imagine in the future someone tries to steal your identity by making a copy of your body, brain, and memories. The copy is identical to you in every way, but they still wouldn't be you. You are still you. That's the selfhood part. It's about the fact that you have been continuously yourself throughout your life.

Here's another problem. What would happen if someone develops more than one identity? Let's say Arthur one day develops a second identity named Martha. Sometimes he's Arthur; sometimes she's Martha. Is Martha real? She has her own personality, desires, and memories. Does she have the right to call herself a person?

Identity can be very confusing!

MORALITY

IS THERE SUCH A THING AS RIGHT AND WRONG?

We all think we know the difference between right and wrong. If you spill some milk, it's right that you clean it up, and it's wrong to leave it for someone else to do. When you're in class, it's right to listen to the teacher and do as you're told, and it's wrong to be noisy and disruptive. Does that mean there are universal rules about right and wrong that we should always follow? Philosophers are divided on this question.

AS A RULE

Plato believed that *morality* (the rules about what's right or wrong) is something that exists separately from human beings, and that it's universal, like mathematics. So Plato would say, for example, that stealing is wrong in the same way that 2 + 2 = 4. This isn't opinion, it's FACT. Plato's approach to morality is known as *objectivism*.

But when you think about it, there's a problem with this. Before there was any life on Earth, there was no goodness or badness. Earthquakes and volcanoes may have destroyed things, but this wasn't right or wrong. The rightness or wrongness of an action must surely depend on its effects on people and animals—whether it causes them pleasure or pain—and also on whether the action is performed by a conscious person.

There's another problem with objectivism—the way actions affect people can vary. Rahul loves celebrating his birthday, whereas Anne doesn't really care about hers. So a rule that says, "You must remember to wish people

a happy birthday," isn't universal like 2 + 2 = 4; it applies to Rahul, but not to Anne.

Even rules such as "do not steal" may not apply all the time. If you're starving to death, would stealing food be wrong? Or if someone is about to detonate a bomb that will kill hundreds of people, is it wrong to kill that person?

As we'll discover in this chapter, it's often very hard to say whether a person's actions are right or wrong. It's often a question of individual circumstances.

Who says what is "right" or "wrong"?

GUT FEELING

Harry thinks that questions of morality should be left up to the individual. He knows in his gut if something's right or wrong. Harry is a *subjectivist*.

The main problem with subjectivism is that it doesn't give a very clear guide about what's right and wrong. At least with objectivism you know where you stand. Objectivists can say things like, "Stealing is wrong," or, "You must always hand in your homework on time." These are clear rules to live by. Harry can only say, "I don't like stealing," and, "I like to hand in my homework on time." For Harry, to say something is "good" only means "I like it."

The trouble is, this ignores the idea of "duty." Harry might not LIKE tidying his room or washing dishes, but an objectivist would say it's still his DUTY to do them. Doing the right thing isn't always the same thing as doing what we like.

Should Harry tidy his room?

There's a third approach to morality, known as *relativism*. This states that morals aren't absolute or up to the individual, but are **shaped by culture**.

For example, in Western countries, tipping a server is regarded as polite, whereas in China it's seen as an insult.

DOING THE RIGHT THING

WHY DO WE BEHAVE WELL?

Why do we try to do the right thing? Is it because we want to make the world a better place? Are we scared of being punished? Or is it because we want people to think we're "good people?" Maybe it's a bit of all of these. Next time you're faced with a choice of doing right or wrong, try thinking about what influenced your decision.

If no one did the right thing, we would live in fear!

TO EACH THEIR OWN

Jamila does what her religion teaches her is the right thing because, as a Muslim, she believes in God and follows the teachings of her *faith*. This is what inspires her to behave morally.

Rahul cares about w*hat other people think of him*. He doesn't want people to think he's a "bad person." That's mainly why he follows the rules and does the right thing.

Maria does the right thing because she would feel very guilty if she didn't. Her *conscience* wouldn't leave her alone.

Oliver has thought logically about why he does the right thing. He believes that if everyone started behaving badly and breaking the rules, society would soon fall apart. If people lied, cheated, stole, or acted violently, no one would trust each other. We'd all end up living in fear behind high walls and thick, padlocked doors. Oliver does the right thing because his *reason* (his ability to think logically) tells him it's the best way for everyone to behave.

CLOAK OF INVISIBILITY

David Hume said our morality doesn't come from our reason, but from our emotions. Harry sees a cat stuck in a tree. It looks very scared. The tree is tall and not easy to climb, but Harry doesn't hesitate—he climbs the tree and rescues the cat! Harry wasn't following any rules when he did this. He wasn't thinking about God or his conscience. He wasn't showing off because there was no one around. He was only thinking about the cat. He felt sorry for it!

The best way of testing your morality is to think about how you'd behave if there was no one around to judge you. Imagine finding an invisibility cloak.

Now you can move around without being seen. Think of all the mischief you could get up to! You could steal from a bank or spy on people and listen in on private conversations. You could scare someone by moving something unexpectedly, or you could trip people you didn't like. No one would ever know it was you. The question is, would you do any of those things? If not, what would stop you?

Plato suggested that we would all be unjust if we had an invisibility cloak. It's only because we aren't anonymous (people know who we are) that we act justly!

What would you do if you were invisible?

JUDGING OUR ACTIONS

WHAT DO YOU THINK?

DOES THE END ALWAYS JUSTIFY THE MEANS?

Jamila knows how much Rahul loves his new jacket, and she knows that he really wants her to like it. The trouble is, Jamila doesn't like the jacket. It's not to her taste at all. Should she lie to spare his feelings, or should she tell the truth? Some philosophers believe the only thing that matters about an action is the amount of goodness or badness it produces. If you do something bad (such as lie about what you think of the jacket), but it produces a good result (makes Rahul happy), that's fine. This philosophy is called *consequentialism*.

ALL ABOUT THE CONSEQUENCES

Not all consequentialists agree on what "good" and "bad" mean. One group called *hedonists* believe that "good" means "pleasure." Another group, the *utilitarians* (see pages 96–97), believe that good means, "The greatest happiness for the greatest number." But what all consequentialists agree on is that the CONSEQUENCE (effect) of an action is all that matters. What motivated it is unimportant.

Florentine philosopher Niccolò Machiavelli (1469–1527) was a consequentialist. He offered advice to rulers on how to use their power. In his book *The Prince,* he argued that rulers often needed to behave cruelly in order to ensure the success and stability of the state. Machiavelli's philosophy has been summarized as, "The end justifies the means."

Consequentialism can sometimes produce results that seem unfair. For example, say Maria visits Harry's house and brings her dog with her. Harry knows how much his mother worries about her priceless vase, so he decides to move it to another room, just in case the dog smashes it. But as he's carrying it there, the dog breaks free of Maria's grasp and leaps on Harry. He drops the vase and it smashes. A consequentialist would say that Harry smashed the vase and so it's his fault. It doesn't matter that Harry's motivation was to try to save the vase.

WELL, YOU MEANT WELL

But philosopher Immanuel Kant would sympathize with Harry in this case. Kant wasn't a consequentialist. He believed that the rightness or wrongness of an action doesn't depend on its consequences, but on its MOTIVATION. This is called *motivism*. So Kant would say that Harry shouldn't be blamed because the MOTIVE of his action was good, even if the result was bad. On the other hand, if Harry had planned to smash the vase but had failed to do so, Kant would say that he should be punished, while a consequentialist would say he shouldn't be.

A moral person, according to Kant, is someone who always acts out of a sense of duty. When deciding what your duty is, he said, act as if you want that act to become a universal law. So he would advise Jamila not to lie to Rahul about the jacket. Otherwise, she'd be suggesting that she thinks lying could be a universal law. No pressure then!

Can rulers justify cruelty if it brings their kingdoms peace?

BY VIRTUE OF ...

A third approach to judging actions is *virtue ethics*. Instead of looking at the consequences or the motivation, these philosophers look at the character traits of those involved. Harry was being caring and thoughtful in protecting his mother's vase. These are virtues, so maybe he should be off the hook!

What do you think?

Is Harry to blame?

HAPPINESS

IS HAPPINESS OUR AIM IN LIFE?

We all like to do things that make us happy and avoid things that make us sad. That's perfectly natural. But is it a good rule to live by? Should happiness be our goal? If so, what is the best way of achieving it? Some people might think it's about seeking pleasure and avoiding pain, but there could be more to it than that.

Chocolate can bring pleasure and happiness, but don't eat too much of it at once, or you might feel pain in the stomach instead!

IGNORANCE ISN'T BLISS

Socrates was one of the first philosophers to look at the question of happiness. He linked happiness to virtue (high moral standards), and believed both could be found through the search for knowledge. This could be done through a process of questioning and reasoning. By the same token, Socrates believed that ignorance was the route to misery and evil.

Aristotle agreed with most of this, but he thought that Socrates didn't pay enough attention to pleasure. No one, according to Aristotle, can be happy without some pleasure in their lives—though he added that moderation is important. Jamila LOVES chocolate, but Aristotle would tell her—enjoy some now and then, but remember that too much can be bad for you.

PLEASURE-SEEKERS

Ancient Greek philosopher Epicurus (341–270 BCE) believed that it was completely normal and natural for people to seek pleasure and avoid pain. He went on to say that pleasure-SEEKING is a good thing—but not every kind of pleasure is healthy. He warned against what he called "dynamic pleasures," such as gluttony (greed for food) and fame, which are usually followed by pain and regret. Instead, he encouraged "passive pleasures" like friendship and good conversation.

Epicurus' philosophy is known as *hedonism*. Hedonists believe that pleasure should be the only aim of all human activity. But critics point out that pain is as much a part of life as pleasure, and sometimes seeking a pleasure like friendship can also lead to pain, such as if a friend dies. Developing skills, creating things, and making friends are worthwhile in themselves and can't be explained as just things that bring us pleasure.

Another criticism of hedonism is that it ignores duty—we often have to do things we'd rather not, such as taking the dog for a walk in the rain when we'd rather be at home in front of the television.

THE SIMPLE LIFE

Not all the ancient Greek philosophers believed that happiness should be the goal of life. Diogenes (*c.*404–323 BCE) rejected all of life's comforts, dressing in rags and living in a barrel. He was the first of a group of thinkers called the *cynics*. They saw the world as fundamentally evil, and believed that the pursuit of material goods—money, fine clothes, good food, and so on—was a worthless activity. Instead, they said, we should lead simple, frugal lives as a way of developing a strong and virtuous character.

"It is impossible to live a pleasant life without living wisely, honorably, and justly, and it is impossible to live wisely, honorably, and justly without living pleasantly." – Epicurus

LYING

IS IT ALWAYS WRONG TO LIE?

Jamila wants the last apple for herself, so she tells Maria there's a worm in it. This is a *lie*. Later, when Jamila bites into the apple, she discovers that there actually is a worm in it! So did Jamila really tell a lie? Can a true statement ever be a lie? Yes—as long as the liar didn't think it was true at the time she said it. When someone says something they BELIEVE to be false in order to DECEIVE another person, they're telling a lie.

WEB OF LIES

Most of us would agree that lying is wrong. But why? What's actually so bad about it?

Well, imagine a world where everyone lied all the time. Life would be really hard! You wouldn't be able to trust what your teachers were telling you at school, or what you learned from books or the Internet. You'd have to find out everything for yourself. Friendships would become almost impossible, as would family life, if you were always worried that people were trying to deceive you.

LIES HURT

Lying hurts the people who are being lied to. It stops them from making informed choices about the future. For example, Oliver wants Anne to go with him to the science museum. Anne would prefer to see a movie. So Oliver tells Anne that the movie stopped showing a week ago. Anne's future will now change—she'll go with Oliver to the museum—because of Oliver's lie.

Lying can also hurt friendships. That evening, Maria mentions to Anne and Oliver how much she enjoyed the movie Anne wanted to see. Anne is upset and angry with Oliver for lying to her. She feels tricked and might find it hard to trust Oliver again in the future.

Lying can hurt both the liars and the people being lied to. Nobody wins!

LIVING IN FEAR

Lying isn't just hard on the people being lied to, but it's also for the liars themselves. Harry once bragged to Rahul that his dad was an astronaut. Rahul told their friends about this, and everyone was really impressed. Now Harry feels he has to keep the lie going— telling them all about his dad's latest trip to the International Space Station! But he's always worried they'll find out the truth. He's stopped inviting his friends over and lives in fear of them spotting his dad in town. Lying can be stressful!

IS LYING EVER OKAY?

Philosophers are divided on this one. Some, like Kant, base their moral thinking on "universal laws." If lying was used everywhere, it would be very harmful. Therefore, Kant concludes, all lying is bad. Others suggest that some lies could be justifiable. Swedish-American philosopher Sissela Bok (born 1934) suggests that before lying, we should ask ourselves if there are any truthful alternatives we could use instead. If not, then we should imagine ourselves in a court of law, and try to justify our lie in front of a jury. What would they think of it?

Before you tell a lie, ask yourself:

"How would you feel if someone told this lie to you?"

THE PURSUIT OF HAPPINESS: JEREMY BENTHAM

Jeremy Bentham (1748–1832) was a British philosopher and reformer (someone who tries to change things for the better). He believed that everything humans do is motivated by two forces—avoiding pain and seeking pleasure. He helped develop a philosophy called *utilitarianism,* **which said that any action should aim for "the greatest happiness for the greatest number." An action's morality should be judged on this aim alone.**

AHEAD OF HIS TIME

As a child, Bentham was extremely bright. He started learning Latin at the age of three and completed his degree at Oxford University aged just 15. After training as a lawyer, he became worried about Britain's criminal justice system and believed that laws and punishments should be changed in a way that would allow the greatest human happiness.

Bentham held unusual beliefs for his time—he wished to ban corporal (physical) punishment and scrap any laws against homosexuals. He also believed in equality for women, animal rights, and votes for all.

Bentham came up with something he called the "felicific calculus," a mathematical formula to help people judge situations. It took into account things like the intensity of pleasure and pain caused by an action, the length of time it lasts, and the number of people affected. He hoped to create a scientific way to assess the rightness or wrongness of any action.

DINNER DILEMMA

Bentham's utilitarian principle—that an action should be judged on whether it achieves the greatest happiness for the greatest number—isn't always easy to use. Maria discovers this when she suggests ordering dinner for delivery …

Maria loves Chinese food but knows that Harry prefers pizza, Anne likes Greek food, and Jamila, Rahul, and Oliver really enjoy Indian cuisine. As a good utilitarian, Maria decides to order from the Indian restaurant. She can't please everybody, but at least this will create the biggest possible amount of happiness. Things get harder, though, when Harry announces he hates Indian food. Now Maria has to weigh up Harry's unhappiness against the happiness of the three who love it.

Some philosophers have criticized utilitarianism for not considering the LONG-TERM effects of people's actions. For example, having children could be seen as bringing great happiness to large numbers of people. But, it could eventually lead to over-population and environmental issues for our planet in the future.

> "Create all the happiness you are able to create; remove all the misery you are able to remove. Every day will … invite you to add something to the pleasure of others—or to diminish something of their pains."
> – Jeremy Bentham

LIVING LIFE

American philosopher Robert Nozick (1938–2002) questioned whether we really are the simple pleasure-seekers that utilitarians assume. He offered a thought experiment to explain otherwise—imagine, he said, that scientists found a way of stimulating someone's brain to give them pleasurable experiences. Once hooked up to this machine, they wouldn't know these experiences weren't real. They could live the life of a rock star, astronaut, or whatever they wanted. But would people really choose this pleasurable fake life over their real lives, however dull or grim those lives are?

Would you choose a fake life of pleasure or a real life of both pleasure and pain?

THE TROLLEY PROBLEM

CAN SAVING FIVE PEOPLE JUSTIFY KILLING ONE?

A train is out of control! You can see it hurtling toward a tunnel. Five people are working in the tunnel, and they're all going to be killed.

You have a lever. If you pull it, you'll direct the train onto a side track, saving the five workers' lives. The trouble is, the side track leads to another tunnel, and one person in there will die if you send the train in that direction. So do you pull the lever or don't you?

DOING NOTHING

This thought experiment, first proposed by British philosopher Philippa Foot in 1967, is known as the "trolley problem." It's especially hard because if you pull the lever, you're making an *active* decision to kill an innocent person.

If you do nothing, you're still making a decision, but a *passive* one. Five people will die, but they would have died anyway, so can you really be held responsible?

TO PULL OR NOT TO PULL

What do the philosophers say? A utilitarian like Jeremy Bentham (see pages 96–97) will always try to maximize happiness and minimize pain. It would minimize the overall pain of the situation to kill one person and save five. So Bentham would advise you to pull the lever.

Immanuel Kant would take a different view. He would say the morality of any action is based on whether the action itself is right or wrong, not the consequences. By pulling the lever, you are effectively murdering an innocent person. Remember that Kant believed we should always try to act as if our action could become a universal law. We would never want murder to become a universal law, so Kant would say we shouldn't pull the lever.

In a survey of philosophers, 68.2% said they would pull the lever, 7.6% said they wouldn't, and 24.2% had another view or could not answer.

SAVING GRACE

In surveys about the trolley problem, most people have said they would pull the lever. This changes though when the problem is changed slightly and they're told that the lone worker on the side track is a member of their family. In this case, far fewer say they would pull the lever. Although many people believe that all humans are equal and that human lives are of equal value, we are far more likely to want to save those close to us than strangers.

One of the surprising things about the trolley problem is that it's a problem at all. Surely it's always better to kill one and save five? The fact that it's not easy proves that we're much more comfortable with letting people die than we are with killing. This can become an issue with very sick people at the ends of their lives. Someone may be in a state of permanent unconsciousness, kept alive by a machine. Yet as long as their life persists, we find it very difficult to switch the machine off, because that would feel like killing them.

Letting someone die feels very different than choosing to kill them.

VIOLENCE

IS IT EVER OKAY TO BE VIOLENT?

Sometimes we see violence on TV. It can be thrilling, tense, scary, or even funny. The actors aren't really fighting, of course. The scene has been created for our entertainment. But violence in real life is nothing like that. It's always horrible. People can get seriously hurt or even killed. Not many people think violence is ever a good thing. But as philosophers, we have to ask ourselves—can violence ever be justified?

AN EYE FOR AN EYE

One justification for violence is when it's used as self-protection. If someone attacks you, most people would say you're allowed to use force to defend yourself. A follower of Kant (see pages 90–91) might call this a DUTY. A utilitarian (see pages 96–97) would look at the CONSEQUENCES—if you did nothing, the pain that your injury or death would cause to yourself and those close to you would be greater than the pleasure it might give to your attacker.

Both would probably say it's okay to defend yourself with reasonable force. The word "reasonable" here is important. If someone punches you in the face, it might be okay to punch them back, but it's not okay to kill them. The violence you use, in other words, must be *proportional* (comparable) to the violence you've received—if you agree it's necessary at all.

KEEPING PEACE

Pacifists are people who believe that violence can never be justified. The most extreme kind of pacifist would say they'd prefer to be killed than to commit a violent act. This might be for religious reasons (they want to keep their soul pure) or because they want to set a moral example for others. These pacifists see their own life as less important than the *principle of non-violence*.

What about when violence is used to protect someone else? If you see someone being attacked by a stronger person, many people would say you have the right to use force to help the victim. This is a more difficult case for the pacifist. It's one thing to say your own life is worth sacrificing for your personal beliefs, but what about someone else's? In the first case, your decision affects only yourself. In the second, it has consequences for another person. An extreme pacifist might argue that the principle of non-violence is worth preserving even if it means the death of an innocent. Less extreme pacifists would say that in such cases violence can be justified.

Superheroes use violence to protect others. Is this right?

WHAT ABOUT WAR?

War is often used as an example of justified violence. Most philosophers distinguish between "just" and "unjust" wars. An *unjust war* might be a war of conquest, where a nation deliberately attacks another nation. *Just wars* almost always involve defending a nation that is under attack. Most people would agree, in such cases, that it's a citizen's duty to support their nation by joining the armed forces or participating in the war effort.

St. Augustine of Hippo (born 354 CE) is known as the founder of the *just war theory*. He believed there were times when it was justifiable to go to war in order to achieve long-term peace.

"A humane person ... will recognize that sometimes the use of violence is a necessary means to a morally worthwhile end, and that moral persons, hating violence in itself, must, under these circumstances, steel themselves to its employment." — Hannah Arendt

QUESTIONING EVIL: HANNAH ARENDT

Hannah Arendt was born into a Jewish family in Hanover, Germany, in 1906. She studied classics and later philosophy at the universities of Berlin and Marburg. In 1933, threatened by the Nazis, she fled to Paris. In 1941, following the Nazi takeover of France, she was held in a prison camp and then forced to flee once again, this time to the USA. In 1961, she visited Jerusalem and witnessed the trial of the notorious Nazi Adolf Eichmann.

SEEING EVIL

As a philosopher, Arendt wrote about *totalitarianism* (a government ruled by a *dictator*, where the people have no freedom), political revolution (removing governments), and what freedom means. In 1963 she published a book about the Eichmann trial: *Eichmann in Jerusalem: A Report on the Banality of Evil*.

Adolf Eichmann had been one of the main organizers of the Holocaust, when millions of Jews were killed in death camps. The Jewish people in countries under Nazi control were rounded up, deported to camps, and worked to death or killed. Eichmann had overseen all of this. After the war, he fled to Argentina, and in 1960 he was captured by the Israeli secret service and brought to Jerusalem to face trial. He was executed in 1962.

THINK AGAIN

Arendt had expected Eichmann to be some kind of monster. Instead, she was surprised to find what an ordinary, everyday sort of man he was. Throughout his trial he claimed he was just following orders, and he did not feel personally guilty for what he had done. Arendt concluded that most of what we call "evil" in this world doesn't come from a desire to hurt, nor from a delight in doing wrong. Instead, it comes from people's failure to THINK about the morality of their actions. Totalitarian regimes like Nazi Germany are able to take advantage of this failure and cause people to do things they wouldn't dream of doing in other circumstances. That way, actions that would usually seem unthinkable become normal.

How do we judge someone for their evil actions?

ORDERS ARE ORDERS

Arendt faced some criticism for this idea. Some said she downplayed the cruelty of the Nazi regime. But Arendt's description of evil as "banal" (ordinary) wasn't intended to take anything away from the horror of what the Nazis did. Instead, it was trying to show that the people who commit terrible acts usually aren't "monsters"—they're mostly ordinary people placed in a situation where "carrying out orders" (however horrible those orders are) seems like the natural thing to do.

This challenges us to ask if we ourselves might be capable of doing evil if we were placed in a similar situation. Arendt said we must always guard against failures in our own thinking and judgement.

"The sad truth is that most evil is done by people who never make up their minds to be good or evil."
— Hannah Arendt

ANIMAL RIGHTS

HOW SHOULD WE TREAT ANIMALS?

Many of us adore animals. We may have a much-loved pet cat or dog, or perhaps we enjoy watching dolphins leaping out of the water, or seeing rabbits hopping around in a meadow. We often feel a strong emotional connection to animals, and this makes us want to be kind to them. But how important is it to be kind to animals, and what form should that kindness take?

BE KIND TO EVERY KIND

Jamila believes that animals have rights. These aren't like human rights, of course. Animals don't need freedom of speech or the right to vote—for obvious reasons! But they do have a right to life, and a right to be allowed to live their lives in peace. A chimpanzee, for example, has intelligence. It can feel joy and sorrow. So, to Jamila, it is no different from a human.

Jamila objects to the way humans use animals for farming, hunting, and entertainment. She doesn't agree with keeping animals as pets (sorry, Maria!)

or in zoos. All these activities, she believes, violate animal rights.

Jamila knows her attitude might not be good news for humans. Some humans might die if animals can't be experimented on to develop new medicines. Humans would also have to adapt to a vegan (no animal products) lifestyle in terms of their diet and clothing. Jamila also accepts that her belief that animals have rights does not apply to very simple life forms like sea cucumbers, worms, or bacteria.

HAPPY AND FREE

Maria doesn't agree with Jamila on this. Animals, she says, don't have rights because they're not moral creatures like human beings. A lion doesn't think about the rights of a gazelle when it kills it, and the gazelle doesn't think its rights have been violated. Because animals have no sense of what rights are, it makes no sense to say they have them.

On the other hand, Maria does believe in animal *welfare*. Humans can make use of animals, so long as the animal doesn't suffer, or its suffering is kept to a minimum. Humans, she says, have a moral duty not to cause them pain or suffering. This isn't because animals have rights. It's because causing pain and suffering is simply wrong.

As a believer in animal welfare, Maria is against many modern farming practices. She wants farm animals to live in good, healthy conditions where they can move around freely, eat a natural diet, and enjoy a life as close as possible to what is natural

Maria loves to keep pets. She just doesn't want them to suffer!

for their species. But Jamila says that it is wrong in principle to farm animals, no matter what kind of conditions they are kept in. It is treating animals as a means to an end (such as human consumption) rather than as creatures with lives that are worth living for their own sake.

"We have to speak up on behalf of those who cannot speak for themselves."
– Peter Singer, *Animal Liberation* (1975)

LEADERSHIP

WHO SHOULD RULE?

"I should be the ruler of our group," says Oliver. "Ruling is a skill, and I've got the best leadership skills." The others don't look too sure about this. "Why should we trust you?" asks Jamila. "Shouldn't we all have a say in decisions?" suggests Maria. "What if we don't agree with your rules?" asks Anne. "Do we even need a leader?" wonders Harry.

THE PHILOSOPHER KING

Deciding who should rule a group may cause a few arguments, but it's not nearly as complicated as deciding who should rule a state. This has been debated by philosophers since ancient times.

Like Oliver, Plato believed that ruling is a skill, and only the skilled should do it. Plato compared "the state" to a human being. Humans, he said, are made up of three elements—*reason* (the logical, thinking part), *spirit* (integrity, anger, and courage), and *appetite* (desires). In a healthy person the three elements are in harmony, with reason, supported by spirit, in control of our appetites. In the same way, a state has three classes—*rulers*, *warriors*, and *citizens*. In a healthy state the all-powerful rulers, supported by the warrior class, will defend the state and keep the citizens under control. Their rule, according to Plato, should be gentle and kind, but firm.

In Plato's ideal society, people showing leadership skills would be selected at an early age to become part of the "aristocracy" (the ruling class). They would get intense training to turn them into "philosopher kings." They wouldn't be allowed to marry or have their own property or wealth, so their only interest would be the public good.

Reason, spirit, and appetite work in harmony to keep a person healthy.

THE PROBLEM WITH POWER

Plato didn't see why people who don't have the "ruling" skill should have any say in the running of the state, which is why he believed in putting power in the hands of the rulers. Other philosophers have criticized this view. First, they say, ruling isn't a science like medicine. There may be just one way to cure a disease, but there are lots of ways to rule a state.

The other problem with having a single, all-powerful ruler is that they would struggle to represent all the different interests of a state. Citizens have their own views of what sort of state they want to live in, and some of these conflict. Jamila wants the group to learn musical instruments and form a band. Maria wants it to be a reading group. Harry would like them to do more sporty activities. If Oliver gets absolute power, he might be tempted to ignore all these views and make the group do only what he wants.

Also, Plato may have misjudged human nature. No matter how well trained a ruler might be, absolute power could easily go to their head. Oliver might soon decide to wear a fancy crown and get the others to bow down before him. He could become a tyrant!

"A true pilot must of necessity pay attention to the seasons, the heavens, the stars, the winds, and everything proper to the craft if he is really to rule a ship."
— Plato, *The Republic*

FEELING FEAR: THOMAS HOBBES

English philosopher Thomas Hobbes was born in Westport, Wiltshire, in 1588, the year that England was attacked by the Spanish Armada. He came into the world earlier than he should have, after his mother heard news of the invading fleet. Hobbes later said, "My mother gave birth to twins: myself and fear." Fear became a major influence on the philosophy that Hobbes went on to develop—fear of the chaos that would come if political authority collapsed.

SURVIVAL OF THE FITTEST

Hobbes earned a degree at Oxford University, then found work as a tutor to the sons of the Earl of Devonshire. He went on to travel across Europe, meeting scientists and philosophers including Galileo Galilei and René Descartes. In 1640, he fled to France to escape the English Civil War. Here, he wrote his great work, *Leviathan*, which set out his ideas about morality, society, and how a state should be governed (ruled).

The violence and chaos of the civil war terrified Hobbes, and he concluded that human beings are basically selfish and egotistical (thinking only of themselves). He imagined an earlier time, before society developed, when humans lived in a "state of nature." In such a savage time, life would have been a battle of each against all, in which only the strongest would win.

Would only the strong survive if everyone was left to fend for themselves?

LAW AND ORDER

Hobbes believed that "society" developed because people realized that, for their own protection, they needed to let go of their selfish instincts and form a "social contract." This was basically an agreement to follow a set of rules, which we now call *laws*. But laws only work if they can be enforced. Hobbes saw the "law enforcer" as a single person with absolute power—in other words, a monarch.

Hobbes gave some liberties to the subjects of this monarch. Since the whole reason people agreed to the social contract was for their own protection, the monarch was not allowed to order subjects to hurt or kill themselves, nor forbid them from defending themselves against others. Subjects couldn't be made to give evidence against themselves in a court of law. Nor did they have to do military service, unless it was to preserve the peace or defend the country against invasion. Other than that, so long as the monarch remained able to protect the subjects, they had to obey him.

The opening illustration of Hobbes' Leviathan shows a monarch's body made up of the people. This expresses his idea that authority is based on the people's consent.

TOO EXTREME?

Philosophers have questioned Hobbes' description of human nature as selfish and egotistical. They've pointed out that people are often kind to others, sacrificing their own interests for those of family, friends, and country. Hobbes seemed so obsessed with keeping peace and order that he was prepared to accept the rule of a tyrant. But surely it's possible to allow the people some freedom without society descending into chaos and civil war?

In a famous phrase, Hobbes described life in the state of nature as being "solitary, poor, nasty, brutish, and short."

PEOPLE POWER

SHOULD THE PEOPLE HAVE A SAY IN HOW THEY'RE RULED?

The friends agree that it wouldn't be fair to give Oliver complete power over them. Instead, Harry says, "Why don't we all rule?" Jamila protests: "That's a recipe for chaos. We need to elect someone to make the rules, and someone else to make sure they're carried out." Jamila knows this is the basic structure of a modern democracy. Her ideas are very similar to those put forward by English philosopher John Locke (1632–1704) when he talked about how the ideal state should be run.

CRIME AND PUNISHMENT

John Locke was much more positive about human nature than Thomas Hobbes (see pages 108–109). His version of the state of nature (life before society) was a lot more peaceful. People owned property and often cooperated with each other. The only problem was there were no laws that everyone could agree on, so when someone hurt or killed another person, or stole from them, the victim would have to take justice into their own hands. People disagreed over what a crime was and how it should be punished.

So "society" developed, according to Locke, because people needed some way of coming up with an agreed set of laws and then enforcing them. But Locke didn't think a monarch should be responsible for this. He thought that if someone tried to gain absolute power over others, it would plunge society into a "state of war."

Could Locke's system lead to the tyranny of the majority?

POWER TO THE PEOPLE

Locke believed that the ultimate source of authority should lie with the people. They should elect (vote in) the government. And he stressed that LAW, not force, should be the basis of that government.

He warned that an absolute monarch could order someone's arrest even when that person hadn't broken a law—when rulers aren't bound by laws, they become tyrants. So, Locke came up with a system of institutions that would share the functions of government. The *legislature* would pass laws, and the *executive* would enforce them. Because the legislature and executive would be appointed by the people, they would be responsible to the people. And because they were separate, they could keep each other in check, and neither would become too powerful. A third branch, the *judiciary*, would judge on individual cases of law-breaking.

MAJORITY RULES

The group decides to try Locke's system of government. Jamila is chosen to be the rule-maker, Oliver is voted rule enforcer, and Maria will judge any cases of rule-breaking. There will be an election every month when the people (Harry, Anne, and Rahul) can decide whether to keep the others in their positions or throw them out. All goes well until Jamila makes a rule that on Wednesday evenings the group will play board games. Harry doesn't enjoy board games, and he objects to the rule. But what can he do about it?

Harry's problem shows a major criticism of John Locke's political theory—the system doesn't serve the interests of individuals or minorities (small groups) in society. In effect, he's replaced the tyranny of the individual with the tyranny of the majority!

LEGISLATURE

EXECUTIVE

JUDICIARY

"Law and not force must be the basis of government. A government which is not based on law is oppressive."
– John Locke

RIGHTS

DO WE HAVE THEM AND WHERE DO THEY COME FROM?

"I have rights!" protests Harry. "And I demand the right not to play board games on Wednesdays!" The others are confused. "If you have rights, then why are you demanding them?" asks Oliver. "I'm not sure there's even such a right as the one you're demanding," says Maria. "Where do rights come from?" asks Rahul.

A RIGHT TO RIGHTS

John Locke (see pages 110–111) was one of the first philosophers to talk about people having *natural rights* (sometimes called *human rights*). He believed there are certain rights we have just by being human, and governments can't interfere with them. He named these our rights to *life, liberty,* and *property.* Locke didn't say exactly where these rights came from, just that they were universal and applied to all people. They aren't the same as "legal rights" (sometimes called "civil rights"), which are given to us through law. An example of a legal right would be the right to vote.

Locke included the right to own property among natural rights because people earn property through their own efforts. He claimed that people had this right to property even before society developed, so society can't take it away from us. Critics have pointed out that people might have claimed property before society existed, but there couldn't have been a natural right to property at that time as there were no laws to uphold that right.

This is an interesting point. How can we say there's such a thing as a natural right when we rely on laws to uphold them? In the state of nature, before society existed, people could injure or enslave us and there would be nothing we could do about it. We could have protested that they were violating our natural rights, but it wouldn't have made any difference at all. So these so-called natural rights are really rights that we've gained thanks to society and the rule of law. Jeremy Bentham actually denied the existence of natural rights and said the only valid rights were legal ones.

Can the right to freedom really be a right when no one is enforcing it?

I DECLARE

In 1948, the United Nations adopted the *Universal Declaration of Human Rights*, a document that set out 30 basic rights for all humanity. These included the right to life, liberty, free speech, and privacy, as well as the right to freedom from torture and the rights to education, social security, and health. The document has inspired governments around the world to create laws to improve the protection of human rights.

The declaration has been praised by many, but has also faced criticism. Some say it does not respect cultural differences. Others have pointed out that some of the rights, such as "the right to rest and leisure, including … holidays with pay" might be a good thing to have, but can't really be described as a universal right.

Philosophers continue to debate what rights are, whether they exist, and, if so, how best to protect them.

What do you think? Do we have natural rights? What rights would you like to see written into law?

TAKING ON TYRANNY: JOHN STUART MILL

John Stuart Mill was born in London, England, in 1806 and became the most influential English philosopher of that century. He worried about the tyranny of the majority and believed a government couldn't call itself "democratic" unless it found a way to protect individuals and minorities.

BREAKING FREE

Mill had a strange upbringing. His father, the philosopher James Mill, gave him an intense education. Shielded from other children his own age, Mill was taught Greek at age three, and by eight was familiar with all the ancient classics. At age 20, after years of strict studying, he had a nervous breakdown. He left education and went to work for the East India Company. Soon, he met Harriet Taylor, a supporter of women's rights. After a twenty-year relationship, she became his wife.

Mill served as a Member of Parliament from 1865 to 1868, putting some of his ideas into practice.

FIGHTING FOR THE LITTLE GUY

In Mill's essay "On Liberty," he showed how to stop a tyranny of the majority.

He realized that tyranny can develop when the public puts pressure on the government. This is exactly how Harry feels. He wants the group to spend Wednesday evenings playing tiring outdoor games. But the members all support Jamila's ruling that they should play board games. They start pressuring the rule-enforcer, Oliver, to kick Harry out of the group if he doesn't go along with the rest of them.

To avoid this sort of takeover, Mill believed that governments should have laws to protect the rights of INDIVIDUALS. The only time a state could be justified in using force against an individual would be to prevent them from harming others. But Harry doesn't seem to be harming anyone. Rahul argues that Harry is harming himself because he's denying himself the joys of board games. Mill would respond—then try to persuade Harry of this, but don't force him against his will!

DIFFERENCE OF OPINION

Harry starts to protest outside. Anne would like to ban him, but Mill would say that Harry has every right to take a stand. He gives two reasons for this:

First, even if the majority opinion is correct, on what basis is that opinion formed? Are they holding it without actually thinking about it, or because they've reached it through debate? By reflecting on and proving wrong all the arguments against your opinion, you actually make it more likely to be correct. Surely it's better to listen to Harry and try to convince him he's wrong than to silence him?

Second, you never know! Harry could be right. Maybe it would do everyone good to get some fresh air and exercise one evening. Or maybe his opinion is partly true. What if the outdoor games could be less tiring? How about making every third Wednesday an outdoor games evening?

"If all mankind minus one were of one opinion, and only one person were of the contrary opinion, mankind would be no more justified in silencing that one person, than he, if he had the power, would be justified in silencing mankind." – John Stuart Mill, *On Liberty*

EQUALITY

SHOULD WE ALL BE EQUAL?

Plato and Hobbes pushed for rule by one person (or a small few). Locke and Mill believed in rule by the people, through democracy. German philosopher Karl Marx (1818–1883) also wanted to see the people rule, but he believed this could only happen through a *workers' revolution*. Marx thought that the economic and political system known as *capitalism* had many weaknesses and was unfair to workers. It needed to be toppled.

A CLASS APART

Capitalism is a system where business is controlled by private owners for profit (to make money). Marx named two main *classes* within capitalism—the *employers*, who own the means of production (the factories, machines, materials, and so on, used in producing goods), and the *workers* they employ. He believed that tension and hatred would build up between these two classes and finally a *revolution* would take place that would lead to a society without any classes.

He was so sure about this prediction, because he believed he'd found a huge problem with capitalism. Marx pointed out that workers produce goods that cost much more than the wages they earn. This "surplus value" (the difference) is not given back to the workers but is kept by the employer as profit. Employers want as much profit as possible, which means paying their workers as LITTLE as possible. Workers, on the other hand, want to earn as much as possible for their efforts. This, says Marx, creates an unavoidable TENSION within capitalism.

The tension is made worse because, in a capitalist system, businesses are always in competition with each other. To make their goods more competitive, each business is under pressure to sell its products as cheaply as possible. Most costs of production, such as tools, machinery, and electricity, are fixed—they can't be cut. The only cost that can easily be reduced is workers' wages.

Does the capitalist system exploit workers?

NONSTARTER

Marx believed the workers would become aware they were being used and would figure out how powerful they could be if they acted together. Revolution would break out, the workers would take over the means of production, and a classless society of freedom and equality would be born.

Critics have pointed out that Marx was wrong in his prediction—capitalism is still the main system to this day. It has survived because it has adapted and changed through the years. Life has improved for workers. Trade unions (workers' organizations) have negotiated better pay and working conditions. And social security systems offer help to people with little or no money coming in.

Since 1917 there have been a number of revolutions around the world inspired by Marx's ideas. But in all cases, these have led to harsh dictatorships that took little notice of human rights. Marx's dream has not come true.

"Let the ruling classes tremble at a Communistic revolution. The proletarians [working class] have nothing to lose but their chains. They have a world to win. Working men of all countries unite!" – Karl Marx, "The Communist Manifesto"

A FAIR SOCIETY

IS IT POSSIBLE TO CREATE A SOCIETY THAT'S FAIR FOR EVERYONE?

"Imagine," says Maria, "that we're all stuck on a desert island. We have to start a society from scratch. How would we organize it?" Harry puts up his hand. "People with names beginning with 'H' should be allowed to do what they like," he smiles. Oliver, the biggest of them, says: "By right of my size, I should eat first. You'd all need me to be strong to fight off wild beasts!" Anne, the oldest, says: "By right of my age, I should have the biggest hut on the island ..."

BACK TO BASICS

Maria's thought experiment was first used by American philosopher John Rawls (1921–2002) in his 1971 book, *A Theory of Justice*. For Rawls, the desert island is an imaginary place where a new society can be founded. It's similar to the "state of nature" used by Hobbes and Locke (see pages 108–111). The people on the island must come together to create a *social contract*. What rules should they set down? As we've seen from Harry, Oliver, and Anne, each person in the new society is going to want to make rules that help themselves, at the expense of others. If they want to create a JUST society that works for everyone, they'll need to think of a different way.

Rawls didn't think a utilitarian system would work (see pages 96–97) because it didn't recognize the importance of the individual. For example, if everyone got slightly more food each day except for Rahul, it would make most of the population happier, but it wouldn't be fair on Rahul. Rawls preferred Kant's idea that each individual in a society is important.

So, Rawls suggested that the group on the island should throw a "veil of ignorance" over their lives: "We need to forget who we are," says Maria. "Forget our names, sizes, ages, talents, and everything else. If we don't know anything about ourselves, we won't know what our personal interests are. We'll be forced to vote for a society that treats everyone fairly."

Rawls thought that if we followed this method, we'd create a society in which each individual is treated fairly and equally, no matter who they are.

LOVELY BUNCH OF COCONUTS

Unlike Karl Marx (see pages 116–117), Rawls wasn't against inequality, but he didn't think very big gaps in equality could be justified. He thought that richer people should only be able to add to their wealth if they could at the same time help the poorest. Say, for example, that Anne becomes the wealthiest on the island because of her grove of coconut trees. If she then discovers a new coconut tree, she can only have it if she agrees to share its coconuts with the island's poorest person, Harry, who has only one coconut tree.

If we try not to see the differences in people, can we create a truly fair society?

Rawls has been criticized by philosophers who point out that people have different natural abilities. Some are stronger, more intelligent, or more creative than others, and any just society cannot ignore these differences. Should such people be denied a greater share of society's benefits?

What do you think?

BIG GOVERNMENT, SMALL GOVERNMENT

HOW POWERFUL SHOULD GOVERNMENTS BE?

Jamila and Oliver have now been elected *governors*. They decide to ban all private businesses on the island. Anne's coconut grove shall from now on belong to everyone, and everyone will have an equal share of its coconuts. Anne is upset about this—she's put a lot of hard work into that grove and it's made her rich! Everyone else is very happy.

IN THE MARKET

As Karl Marx said (see pages 116–117), capitalism can create a very unequal society. The *free market* (businesses competing with each other) can lead to lots of wealth ending up in the hands of just a small number of people. Should governments be allowed to interfere in the free market to try to make society more equal? Most people think governments have some role to play, such as by making businesses pay taxes to help pay for public services, and making sure workers are fairly treated. But there's a lot of disagreement about how much power governments should have to interfere in economic life.

Karl Marx is at one extreme. He believed that after a workers' revolution, there would need to be an all-powerful government in charge. He called it a

"dictatorship of the proletariat (working class)." This worker-led government would take over every business, ending all private enterprise. He imagined that the government would eventually "wither away," ushering in a new era he called *communism*. Then there would be no classes, and society's wealth would be owned by everyone.

But in all the communist revolutions that Marx inspired, the all-powerful government never withered away. As the only owner of the country's businesses, the government made all the goods and set all the prices. This never works well. The government-run economies of communist countries tend to become very inefficient, often leading to shortages of important goods.

SOMEWHERE IN THE MIDDLE

At the other extreme are the *libertarians*. Libertarianism is a philosophy that emphasizes the freedom of the individual above anything else. Libertarians believe that individuals have the right to live, work, and do business as they please, without interference from the government. So the libertarians would be on Anne's side.

Scottish economist and philosopher Adam Smith (1723–1790) is a hero to many libertarians. He was the first to show that SENSIBLE self-interest of businesspeople in a free market, without government interference, can actually lead to wealth and prosperity for all.

It's certainly true that free-market capitalism has helped lift billions of people out of poverty in places like China and India. But, it has also caused huge income inequality and harsh conditions for workers in countries where these workers don't have government protection.

Today, most people support the idea of a *capitalist* economic system working within rules set by governments.

"It is not from the benevolence of the butcher, the brewer, or the baker that we expect our dinner, but from their regard to their own interest." — Adam Smith, *The Wealth of Nations*

WHAT KIND OF FREEDOM?

SHOULD WE BE FREE TO MAKE BAD CHOICES?

Jamila is cycling through town. She arrives at a road where she can turn left or right. She hesitates for a moment, then decides to turn left. No one told her which way to go. She was completely free to make her choice ... Or was she? To understand why she might not have been free to make that choice, we need to look inside her head at the moment she made her decision.

Jamila is torn between a good choice and a bad choice.

DRIVEN BY A CRAVING

Jamila is on her way to audition for a band she really wants to join. The house where the band is meeting is to the right. But as she reaches the turn, she gets a sudden craving for ice cream. The shop that sells ice cream is to the left. She knows that going to buy ice cream will make her late for the audition, but she goes anyway.

One definition of the word "free" is to be in control of your actions in order to pursue your own interests. Jamila really wants to join this band, but she's unable to pursue this interest because of her craving for ice cream. So it sounds like she isn't actually free in this sense of the word. There's nothing physically stopping her though—it's coming from within herself.

FREE RIDE

Russian-British philosopher Isaiah Berlin (1909–1997) said there are two kinds of freedom—*positive freedom* (the ability to take control of your life and achieve your goals) and *negative freedom* (the absence of external obstacles or barriers). Jamila has negative freedom. There are no obstacles on her cycle journey. What she doesn't have is positive freedom to make the right choice for herself about which way to turn.

Libertarians (see pages 120–121) believe the only freedom that a government should protect is negative freedom—the government should take away all external obstacles from citizens so they're free to act as they please. Whether Jamila chooses to go to an audition or buy ice cream should be entirely up to her, and nothing to do with the government.

There are others, however, who think government should play a role in promoting the positive freedom of citizens. This is called *social liberalism*. Social liberals see it as part of a government's duty to promote healthy lifestyles and discourage harmful choices, so that citizens are better able to achieve their goals. For example, a socially liberal government might run campaigns encouraging people to do more exercise or eat healthy food. They might regulate, tax, or even ban the use of products or activities considered harmful, such as cigarettes, gambling, and sugary foods.

Libertarians argue that by banning or restricting these things, governments are actually taking freedom away from citizens. They believe that adult citizens should be free to choose for themselves whether they want to buy these products and take part in these activities, even if they're bad for them.

Should the government nudge Jamila in the right direction?

What do you think?

Should the government help Jamila make a good choice for her, or is it up to her to choose badly?

DO WE NEED A GOVERNMENT?

COULD WE LIVE WITHOUT RULERS?

"Maybe we don't actually need rules, or rulers," says Harry. "We could just do what we like as individuals." The others aren't sure about this idea. Oliver thinks it would cause chaos, Maria worries the group might fall apart, and Anne fears they'd end up doing nothing! But could Harry be right? Can small groups, or even whole countries, work without rules or rulers?

OUTSIDE OF THE LAW

The idea that societies don't need governments or laws is called *anarchism*, and it has a long history. Diogenes and Epicurus (see pages 92–93) didn't think much of political authority. Diogenes scraped the faces off coins as an act of rebellion. Epicurus told his followers to step away from society and avoid living under its laws.

On the other hand, Thomas Hobbes described the anarchic "state of nature" as a terrifying, chaotic place when he was justifying the need for strong government.

But British philosopher William Godwin (1756–1836) argued that government itself brings about its own kind of unhappiness. Governments, he said, tend to be "despotic" (tyrannical).

Maria worries that if they follow Harry's suggestion, they'll have nothing to keep them together, and the group will fall apart. But anarchists argue that an anarchic society doesn't have to be like that. Successful anarchic communities have been established where there's no leader and no rules, and members still feel they belong to a strong group. They support each other because they want to, not because anyone's telling them to. The French political thinker Pierre-Joseph Proudhon (1809–1865) supported the idea of anarchic communities where all wealth is shared and there is no private property.

NEVER STOP THINKING

Rahul fears that if they have no rules, people will take advantage. Someone might steal all the coconuts, or refuse to clean the hut when it's their turn. He has a point. For an anarchic community to work, everyone has to work together for the common cause. As John Rawls (see pages 118–119) said, everyone must forget self-interest and think only of the interests of the group.

Oliver predicts that their experiment in anarchism won't last. "People need rules," he says. Robert Nozick (see pages 96–97) argued something similar. He believed that government would always come out of anarchy. People would buy protection from another individual or group in order to feel secure, and this "protection agency" would eventually turn into a government.

Despite these worries and warnings, the group agree to give Harry's idea a try. As Jamila says, "Even if it doesn't work, it's always worth trying something new!"

She's right. The point of philosophy is never to be scared of fresh ideas. Always be ready to explore new ways of thinking—ask questions, debate them with your friends, and keep an open mind.

"It is earnestly to be desired that each man should be wise enough to govern himself." —William Godwin

GLOSSARY

abstract

Not real but existing as a thought or idea.

belief

An idea that may not be real but which is accepted as true, often without proof.

capitalism

A system where businesses are controlled by private owners for profit.

concept

An idea that you cannot see or touch, but can hold in your mind, like numbers or a unicorn.

consciousness

Your awareness—the sum of your mind, thoughts, and feelings.

consequences

The results or effects of how we act and what we do.

dictator

A ruler who has complete power, and who has usually taken control by force (or the threat of force).

duty

Something you must do, either because you are told to or because you believe you should.

exist

To be real, to be present as a fact that cannot be denied.

experience (noun)

A situation that leaves an impression on you. Also, the knowledge gained by doing.

experience (verb)

To be in a situation, or have a feeling about it.

faith

Strong belief, often in a particular religion.

freedom

Being able to do, speak, and think as you like, unaffected by anyone or anything else.

free will

The power to make your own choices in life, without being influenced by God or fate.

hedonist

Someone who believes that the most important thing in life is to seek pleasure.

illusion

An idea that is wrong or false, or something that only seems to be real or which is actually something else.

imagine

To form an idea or a picture in your own mind. What you can imagine may not be real, like a unicorn.

individual

A single person (or thing), separate from a group.

infinite

Being without limits or an end, and so impossible to measure.

justification

A good reason or explanation for something that exists or which has happened.

knowledge

Certain understanding, gained

by reasoning or from experience or learning.

logic

A way of reasoning step by step. Each step must be true to lead to the next step.

mind

The part of you that lets you think and reason.

morality

The system of principles concerning how we behave and choose between doing right and wrong.

paradox

A statement that seems to be unlikely or even impossible to be true, often because it is in conflict with itself.

perception

Being aware of something through your senses, especially your sight.

principle

A rule, belief, or theory for governing how we, or things, behave.

reality

The state of things as they are and as they happen. Some philosophers believe reality is imagined.

reasoning

Thinking about something in a careful, step-by-step way to reach a conclusion.

rights

What you may do or have, because either the law allows you, or moral principles do.

self

The part of you that makes you *you*—and different from anyone else.

skeptic

Someone who questions or doubts ideas that many others accept as true.

society

The people living in a particular region, sharing laws and organizations, and following a similar way of life.

state of nature

The way we lived before we created society.

truth

Being correct, just like in reality, and with no possibility of doubt.

utilitarian

Someone who believes that actions are right when they benefit most people.

virtue

A good way of behaving, action that is right (and avoids wrong).

INDEX